F***
My Life

F****
My Life

And You Thought You'd
Had a Bad Day …

Maxime Valette, Guillaume Passaglia
and Didier Guedj

Illustrations by Andrew Pinder

Michael O'Mara Books Limited

Published in Great Britain in 2009 by
Michael O'Mara Books Limited
9 Lion Yard
Tremadoc Road
London SW4 7NQ

First published in the United States of America in 2009 as *F My Life: It's Funny, It's True, Except When It Happens to You*. Some material originally published in France by Michel Lafon in 2008.

Published by arrangement with Villard, an imprint of The Random House Publishing Group, a division of Random House, Inc.

A CIP catalogue record for this book is available from the British Library.

Papers used by Michael O'Mara Books Limited are natural, recyclable products made from wood grown in sustainable forests. The manufacturing processes conform to the environmental regulations of the country of origin.

ISBN: 978-1-84317-414-1

1 3 5 7 9 10 8 6 4 2

www.mombooks.com

Designed by Burville-Riley Partnership

Printed and bound in Great Britain by Clays Ltd, St Ives plc

CONTENTS

AUTHORS' ACKNOWLEDGEMENTS

Our thanks go to:

Julien Azarian, Alan Holding, Frans van Schoor, Marielle Bonnard, Isabelle Abraldes, Camille Bourély, Gawelle Serré and Laura Cherfi, for their everyday involvement in the FMyLife adventure.

Maxime, Guillaume and Didier, 2009

INTRODUCTION: A SHORT HISTORY OF FML

It all started in a chat room in France. A few friends got into the habit of telling each other the crappy things that had happened to them that day ... a process that eventually, in January 2008, became a blog named www.viedemerde.fr ('Shitty Life').

As interest in these stories began to reach a wider audience, the website grew and grew. In time, we knew that we had to welcome the English-speaking world on board our mission.

www.fmylife.com now has visitors from across the globe; 123 million hits and counting. After its launch, we quickly realized something fascinating: the same kind of shitty events occur all over the world, every day, to all sorts of people. There is a kind of solidarity among all countries when it comes to misfortune. We are all flailing around in a big, international pile of crap. We are in it together.

The idea is simple: people share their shameful experiences, describing in just a few sentences the absolutely horrible and horrific moments that have ruined their day. Think of it as: 'Life's a bitch – and then you email FMyLife.' Each entry begins with 'today' and ends with '**FML**'.

Laughing at others' adversities is a time-old tradition – after all, one man's misery is another man's mirth. This is schadenfreude on a supersized scale. The anecdotes span all sorts of topics, such as money, love, work, sex, kids, and more. The full spectrum of life is here in all its devastating glory. And as with life, some of the entries are dark. Very dark. Others are as slapstick as a circus show.

Wondering if they're true? They are. A good **FML** is something you just can't make up. In *F∗∗∗ My Life*, the book, we've sifted through our classic collection to bring you the best of the worst: the most heartbreaking and the most hilarious.

Without a doubt, Maxime is to blame for coming up with the original concept, and then the French website. Guillaume later joined him to help out, and then Didier was asked to become part of the FMyLife adventure. We'd all like to thank the thousands of people who have had the requisite sense of humour and self-deprecation to send us their tales of trouble and strife. It's become a real gold mine of embarrassment, and it's amazing.

Of course, working in such a huge mine means you have to push that little bit harder to extract the real gems – but the joy of finding a new, funny story makes this the best job in the world. This really is pure gold, people – keep it up!

Enjoy!

THE SHAME OF IT

Today, I was at work in a supermarket and a woman pushed her trolley over to my checkout. It was filled with crisps, bread, dips and drinks. I said to her, 'Looks like you're going to have a fun party.' She then looked at me and said, 'My mother just died – this is for after the funeral.' **FML**

Today, I ate at a friend's house. Her five-year-old son, who was at the table with us, looked at me and said quietly, 'You're ugly!' When my friend came back, I told her what had happened. She scolded him briefly and then the boy began to cry, shouting, 'But she isn't pretty!' **FML**

*

Today, my boyfriend was lying on top of me and he was looking at me with passionate eyes. I thought he was finally going to tell me he loved me. But instead he said, 'You have a bogey.' **FML**

*

Today, I saw the following message on my Facebook News Feed: 'Morning Sex: [My mum] and [My dad] are fans. Click here to join.' **FML**

Today, I saw a few old colleagues at a bar. They recognized me and started calling me by the nickname they had for me, of which I was unaware. It appears I was known to the entire office as 'Butch Megan' for two whole years. **FML**

*

Today, thinking I was being very generous, I lent my jacket to my new colleague. Maybe I should have checked my pockets first. I'm not sure that having three different flavours of condoms made a good impression. **FML**

Today, I was in Spain, and I told the kids I was teaching that I was excited to be working with them. Only the form of excitement I used apparently refers to sexual excitement. I told the kids I was sexually aroused to be working with them. **FML**

Today, I got two text messages from my girlfriend. The first was to tell me it was all over; the second was to say she'd sent it to the wrong person. **FML**

*

Today, I looked at the Facebook page of the girl I really like, and saw that she had recently written on her friend's wall: 'Last night was the biggest mistake of my life.' We hooked up last night. **FML**

Today, while I was out having a drink with a pretty girl, she started looking at my crotch and said smilingly, 'There's something burning down there.' I grinned, but she insisted. Ashes had set my trousers on fire. **FML**

Today, when I woke up, my husband was already out of bed. Thinking I heard him padding by in the hall, I shouted out, 'Get that cock in here right now!' A voice replied, 'He's gone out to get some bread.' It was my mother-in-law. **FML**

✱

Today, I put my hand up in class. I forgot that I hadn't shaved my armpits. **FML**

✱

Today, a child sitting next to me on the bus pointed at me and asked: 'Mummy, when it's not a man and it's not a woman, what is it then?' **FML**

Today, I accidentally walked in on my girlfriend masturbating, so I said to her, 'Need a hand with that?' To which she replied, 'I'm doing fine here on my own, don't ruin it.' **FML**

*

Today, I had a job interview at a new restaurant. One manager asked me why I should be hired. I said I was more efficient than most. I left to find I'd locked my keys in the car. It took all the managers to help me get my keys out. **FML**

*

Today, I decided to practise putting a condom on with my mouth. Then my flatmate walked in on me using my mouth to roll a condom onto a banana. **FML**

Today, I had my first meeting with my new bosses. For lunch, we went to a restaurant. I choked on a piece of meat and couldn't breathe. I had to take the chunk of meat out of my throat with my fingers, and then put it back on my plate all chewed up. **FML**

Today, I played in a tennis tournament. After winning, I went to shake my opponent's hand. He didn't react or move. It was only the first set. **FML**

Today, I was walking through town with my girlfriend when we passed a group of Brownies selling home-baked biscuits. I saw they had my favourite kind, oatmeal and raisin, so I pointed at them and shouted, 'Yeah!' at the top of my voice. My girlfriend looked shocked. Behind the cookies was a five-year-old Brownie bent over, with her bottom pointing at me. **FML**

✱

Today, I had an interview for a job. During the interview, my phone rang. My ringtone is the *Teletubbies* theme. **FML**

✱

Today, I made love to my girlfriend. I penetrated her for a while, then stopped to get my breath back. She carried on moaning, even though I'd stopped moving. **FML**

✱

Today, I dressed in my sexiest clothes (Gucci and Prada, worth a real fortune) to meet my new boyfriend at a restaurant. As I was a bit early, I took the opportunity to smoke a cigarette outside, by the front door, while I was waiting. The restaurant owner then came out and said, 'Hey, you, go and "work" somewhere else, please.' **FML**

✱

Today, to amuse my girlfriend, I put on her sexy nightie and went out on the balcony for a smoke, wriggling about in front of her window. She laughed until one of her neighbours shouted, 'Hello!' from the upper floor, grinning at the show. **FML**

Today, I woke up to my wife talking in her sleep: 'No, Brandon! I don't want to have sex!' My wife won't have sex with me when she's awake or in her dreams. **FML**

*

Today, at a rehearsal, a friend poked me: 'My mother is in the orchestra – guess who she is!' I jokingly answered, 'Umm … The fat singer?' It was. **FML**

*

Today, at the supermarket, everybody was staring at me. After ten minutes, I realized that my umbrella was still open. **FML**

*

Today, my wife and I went to a wedding. At one in the morning (when the cheese was being served), we were starting to fall asleep at the table, so we went to our car to take a short nap. When we woke up, at about 5 a.m., the party was over. **FML**

*

Today, it's been two weeks since I lost my virginity and I've already had sex with three guys. **FML**

*

Today, I received a really nice set of red satin underwear, with a bra, a thong and a corset … from my grandfather. **FML**

Today, I called my girlfriend and she answered telling me how amazing the sex was last night and that she can't wait to see me later. I didn't see her last night. **FML**

*

Today, I fell asleep on the train, totally wiped out after a party the night before, which had involved lots of booze and very spicy Indian food. When I woke up, I noticed a small boy on the seat in front staring at me. I smiled at him, and then he turned to his father and said, 'Daddy, the farting man just woke up.' **FML**

Today, I'm a med student, in my sixth year, and I have spent the whole day in surgery. No one told me that what I was wearing on my feet was actually supposed to be put over my hair. **FML**

Today, my watch broke, so I mentioned to my dad that I needed a new one. A little while later, he hands me a really nice watch. He says, 'Here, this one's been lying around for a while.' It was his Father's Day present. **FML**

*

Today, I discovered that my fiancé had tried to fake his own death because he thought it would be easier than confessing to the affair he was having. **FML**

Today, a colleague and I walked out of our office at the same time. He got in his car, which was parked right outside. I asked him what I had to do to get a sweet parking spot like that. He proceeded to roll up his trouser leg and show me his prosthesis. He was in the disabled spot. **FML**

Today, I got caught stealing lollipops. I am twenty-five. **FML**

Today, I thought I was going on a date. About twenty minutes into it, after giving her my arm to hold like a true gentleman, it came up in conversation that my brother is gay. Her response: 'Oh, so both you and your brother are gay?' **FML**

Today, my boyfriend and I were looking for our bubblegum-flavoured 'numbing' lotion to have some morning fun. We couldn't find it anywhere. About ten minutes later, my little nephew appeared, crying, with drool coming out of his mouth. He smelt like bubblegum, and his mouth and tongue were all numb. **FML**

*

Today, as I came out of a changing room, I gave back all the stuff I'd tried on to a saleswoman. I then walked off, but after a couple of steps I changed my mind and decided to purchase one of the items. When I got back, the saleswoman was spraying the changing room I'd used with deodorant. **FML**

*

Today, my mother called to say that my eleven-year-old nephew had found my secret stash of nipple tassels, furry handcuffs, and a bottle of lube. He doesn't want to visit me anymore. **FML**

*

Today, I got together with a small group of friends at a bar. I went up to order a drink, but with all the music and noise, the bartender couldn't hear what I was trying to say, so he leaned forward, cocking his ear towards me. I thought he was being very friendly, so I kissed him. **FML**

*

Today, I was at an interview for a music school. I got my guitar out of its case, and realized that my friends thought it would be very funny to replace my real guitar with one from *Guitar Hero*. **FML**

Today, while on a date with the guy of my dreams, I cut my tongue so badly it bled for an hour. I cut it on the plastic spoon from my coffee. **FML**

*

Today, I went home for my grandma's ninety-fifth birthday. While there, she noticed my new tongue piercing and asked why I would get it done. Before I could reply, my cousin said, 'So she can make the boys happier when she's sucking on them.' She's nine years old. **FML**

*

Today, I had to give a speech on stage at a local preschool about fire safety. I'm thirty-two years old and passed out on stage because I felt extremely nervous and intimidated by a group of four-year-olds. **FML**

*

Today, I was sitting on the couch, my computer next to me and my dick in my hand, when my flatmate walked in. Scared and looking me right in the face, he says, 'What's for dinner?' **FML**

*

Today, in class, I asked my teacher for a 'rubber'. I didn't realize that, in America, 'rubber' doesn't mean 'eraser' – it means 'condom'. **FML**

*

Today, three girls introduced themselves to me. I had met all of them before. **FML**

Today, I was studying abroad in Mexico and someone asked me what it was like to be from England. I responded in Spanish, in front of thirty people, with what I thought translated to: 'If you get cold, you can just put on a jacket.' Apparently, what I thought meant 'jacket' actually means 'masturbate'. **FML**

*

Today, I was a host at a kids' event. I started to do some funny moves to entertain the kids. I was wearing a low-cut top. Then I noticed that all the children were pointing at me, and the adults looked shocked. Both my boobs had popped out. **FML**

*

Today, I sang the 'Itsy Bitsy Spider' song with a class of thirty twenty-somethings because we're going to be preschool teachers. Our tutor made us do the hand motions, too. **FML**

Today, I went to the gym to try to get into shape. I pulled a muscle taking off my sweater in the locker room. **FML**

Today, my nephew asked me how babies are made. I thought he'd had this chat with his mum, but I went into it again. After a twenty-minute 'discussion', he said, 'So what about the good stuff – get to the blow jobs and the lesbians.' He's eleven. **FML**

*

Today, my girlfriend caught me picking my nose and eating the bogey. **FML**

*

Today, my best friend was crying because her boyfriend is an idiot. I brought my thumb up to wipe a tear off her face, and somehow stuck it up her nose. **FML**

*

Today, I farted a lot during my exam, but they were all silent so I figured I should be OK. Then I looked around and everybody was suffocating and giving me sly looks. I am now known to everyone in the department as 'Super Fart'. **FML**

*

Today, at work, a man walked up the escalator with his chubby kid next to him and asked me where the shoes were. I said, 'For you or your son?' He said, 'For my daughter.' **FML**

*

Today, my biology teacher was putting together a skeleton model for the class. He had misplaced the leg bone, so I thoughtfully asked, 'What's the matter, lose a leg?' Unfortunately, there's nothing funny about asking that question of a guy with an amputated leg. **FML**

Today, I went to my parents' house for dinner. When I got there, I noticed that they had gay-pride flags hanging from the porch, and gay-rights bumper stickers plastered to their cars. There was also a huge 'We accept you, Nick' banner hanging from the garage. I'm not gay. **FML**

*

Today, my girlfriend of one month and I had an amazing night of dinner and dancing, but when I leaned in to kiss her, she said, 'You're joking, right?' **FML**

Today, my girlfriend and I had sex for the first time. When I was on top of her, she asked me if it was in yet. I said yes. She sighed. **FML**

Today, my friends and I went to a bar and proceeded to get wasted. I was walking around and saw a kid. I started yelling, 'There's a child in this bar! There's a CHILD in this BAR!' She turned around. She was a little person. **FML**

*

Today, I accidentally unplugged my headphones in the quiet section of the library, causing my music to play from my laptop at full volume. I was listening to Celine Dion. I'm the captain of the football team. **FML**

Today, I'd just finished having sex with my girlfriend when she asked if I had started smoking weed again. I said yes and asked if she could smell it on me, since I had recently smoked. She replied, 'The only time you can last that long is when you're high.' **FML**

*

Today, the guy I fancy talked to me for the first time. He told me to stop staring. **FML**

*

Today, I was at church and saw a blind teenager who obviously felt lost. Feeling like I should help, I went over and asked if he needed anything. He said, 'I can't find my carer.' I asked, 'What does she look like?' **FML**

*

Today, I went in for my second day at my new job. My bosses greeted me and told me we were going to have a meeting. The meeting was to listen to the drunk voicemails I left them on Saturday. **FML**

*

Today, my husband found the box my morning-after pill came in. He had a vasectomy ten years ago. **FML**

*

Today, I was working at a supermarket. A kid about five years old was having trouble zipping up his jacket. I reached out to help him and he started screaming, 'No bad touch bad touch!' and kicked me in the knee. Everyone looked. **FML**

Today, I was getting it on with a girl in my apartment and I told her I didn't have a condom. She responded by laughing in my face. Upon realizing my look of confusion, she said, 'Oh, you actually thought I'd have sex with you?' **FML**

*

Today, I fell asleep in my driver's ed class, and woke up in the middle of a dream, laughing. Everyone stared at me. I later found out that the teacher had just finished talking about his vegetative niece who didn't wear a seat belt. **FML**

*

Today, I was instructed by my boss to welcome the two new foreign business partners, since I am the only one who can speak their language. When they arrived, I greeted them in their language. One of them scratched his head and asked his companion in plain and clear English, 'What did he say?' **FML**

*

Today, in front of the entire family, I yelled at my mum and told her she wasn't a good parent. She replied, 'Well, at least I had friends when I was your age.' **FML**

*

Today, while I was walking through the perfume section in a shop, a woman behind me asked, 'Excuse me, miss, would you like to sample our new fragrance line?' I'm a nineteen-year-old male. I turned around, expecting her to correct herself. She didn't. **FML**

Today, I was making love with my girlfriend and my landline rang. Obviously, I let it go to answerphone. At the very moment I was about to come, I heard my mum's voice on the machine: 'Hi, sweetheart.' **FML**

*

Today, I went out to dinner with my family. I was given a kids' menu when the waitress sat us down. I'm twenty-four. **FML**

*

Today, my four-year-old cousin gave me a hug, basically stuffing his face into my crotch. Then he pulled it out and said, 'Ew, that's stinky,' in front of my entire extended family. **FML**

*

Today, when I threw my cigarette out of the car window, the wind blew it back in again. My trousers got completely burnt. **FML**

Today, I was in the car with a group of my friends, discussing sexual experiences, when I looked down and realized my BlackBerry had dialled the family I babysit for – and left a five-minute voicemail. **FML**

Today, in the middle of a dinner date, I went to rest my chin on my hand, missed, and stuck the straw from my drink straight up my nose. I bled all over the table. He hasn't called me since. **FML**

*

Today, at church, the little boy sitting behind me asked his mother if I had chickenpox because there were red dots all over my face. I've had bad acne since I was twelve. **FML**

*

Today, I was talking to the guy I fancy about making the girls' football team. Excited, he congratulated me and asked for my number. I proceeded to give him my mobile number. He laughed and said, 'Your shirt number.' **FML**

*

Today, after I had filled up my car and got into it, I saw a hot guy running towards me. I flashed a smile and left the door open. He said, 'The pump is still attached to your car – you really should be more careful.' **FML**

*

Today, I got a 'save the date' card for the wedding of a couple my husband knows. I was excited because I really want to be better friends with these people. I emailed the bride – 'I got your STD!' – and hit send before I realized how that sounded. **FML**

*

Today, my mum decided to introduce me to her new boyfriend. I know him. I've slept with him. **FML**

Today, I went to a plastic surgeon with a friend. The doctor walked in and, without looking at his notes, started explaining the liposuction procedure to me. I had to interrupt him to tell him that I was only there to support my friend's nose job. **FML**

*

Today, my group of friends, my girlfriend and I were playing 'Never Have I Ever'. My girlfriend's turn came up and she went with, 'Never have I ever had an orgasm.' **FML**

*

Today, while at the Golden Gate Bridge, I spotted a large group of Asian people trying to take a group shot. Trying to be helpful, I slowly said, 'You ... want me ... take picture?' while using hand gestures. The man looked at me and said, 'No thanks, asshole, I got it,' in perfect English. **FML**

*

Today, I decided to brush up on my flirting skills and asked a guy I fancy what time it was. He pointed to the very visible watch on my wrist and said, 'You should know already.' **FML**

*

Today, my parents met my boyfriend's parents for the first time. Bailing us out of jail. **FML**

*

Today, my professor, who was born without arms, asked somebody, 'Need a hand?' There are over 300 students in that class and I was the only one laughing. **FML**

Today, I was DJing at a wedding. The groom wanted a song played for his grandma and grandpa. I requested over the microphone that his grandparents come to the dance floor for a special song. Turns out they've been dead for over a year and the song was supposed to be in dedication. **FML**

✱

Today, I was having sex with my girlfriend for the first time, and she asked me if I ever get made fun of in the locker room for my small penis. **FML**

✱

Today, I was interviewing a gorgeous guy for my journalism class, and he asked to borrow my laptop to check his email quickly. After the interview, I realized that the last thing I had searched for on Google was 'ingrown pubic hairs' – and it was still up there. **FML**

✱

Today, at a party, I told this guy that I really liked his pirate costume. Turns out he wasn't wearing a costume – his eye was shot out with an air rifle. This explains the eyepatch. **FML**

✱

Today, my brother and I were role-playing in a medieval setting, when suddenly he took off all of his character's clothes and said, 'Let's have sex!' I looked at him and said, 'Uh, you are my brother!' He then turned to me, smiling, and replied, 'But not in the game!' I am a nineteen-year-old girl. He is twelve. **FML**

Today, I drove to a job interview. I had to sneeze, but because I was driving on the motorway, I didn't let go of the wheel to cover my nose. I didn't know the sneeze was a 'productive' one until I was sitting in the interview, looked down at my new blouse and saw the giant ball of snot sitting there. **FML**

*

Today, I went on the best date I've been on in years. Later on, over drinks, we get talking and I explain how I came out to my friends and family. When I ask him how he came out, he replies that he isn't gay and, oh, did I think this was a date? **FML**

*

Today, I took the train to college. The man across from me would not stop staring at my breasts. Finally, the train came to my stop. As I got up, I said, 'Nothing to see now, wanker.' Then I noticed his white walking stick, as he got up to get off too. He was blind. **FML**

*

Today, I went to the hairdressers and asked how much it was for a haircut, shampoo and blow job. I meant to say blow dry. **FML**

*

Today, I was in my Spanish class, having a debate about the death penalty. When I went to make a point, I meant to say, '*La pena de muerte*,' which means 'the death penalty'. I said, '*La pene de muerte*.' Turns out that means 'the penis of death'. **FML**

Today, I forgot to do my French homework, but since it was an online worksheet, I told my teacher my Internet wasn't working. I told her via email. **FML**

Today, as I walked out of the toilets, two guys checked me out and said, 'Nice tail.' I smiled and strutted to my next class. When I went to sit down at my desk, the girl behind me said, 'Did you know you have toilet paper hanging out of your pants?' **FML**

Today, I was babysitting a one-year-old. She's just learned how to say 'yes', so if you ask her anything, she'll say 'yes'. I asked her if she liked vegetables and she said, 'Yes!' Then I asked her if I was pretty. She looked at me and said, 'No.' **FML**

Today, I met this really attractive guy who introduced himself as Wyan. He was really cool and sweet and we got along pretty well. Later, someone told me that his name is Ryan and that he has a speech impediment. The whole conversation I had been referring to him as Wyan. **FML**

✱

Today, I was in my room and I drew a *Harry Potter* lightning bolt on my forehead in eyeliner, just because it cheers me up. Then some friends came over randomly, so we went out to get a drink, and when I got back I realized the lightning bolt was still there. I'm at college. **FML**

Today, I was typing up a love letter on my computer. A sexual love letter. I was in a classroom, I'm the teacher, I'm gay, and my love letter showed up on the whiteboard while my students were taking a test. It was up there for fifteen minutes. **FML**

Today, I was meeting friends for dinner at an Indian restaurant. I was waiting for the group to arrive and our table to be ready. An Indian man approached me, smiling, so I said, 'We're not ready for our table yet.' Then I realized it was my friend's boyfriend, whom I've met several times before. **FML**

Today, I was sitting beside this handsome guy on a bench. Suddenly, he says, 'I know we don't know each other very well, but would you like to have dinner on Saturday?' I turn to him with a goofy smile, and exclaim, 'I'd love to!' He gives me a weird look, turns his head and points to his phone. **FML**

*

Today, my friend and I went to a tacky themed party. She was wearing orange, faux snakeskin stilettos. I commented, 'Those are perfect for tonight – where did you manage to find such hideous shoes?' It turns out she wears those shoes all the time – the colour just matched her outfit. **FML**

*

Today, I hit a parked car. I was walking. To make the scene more embarrassing, the car alarm shocked me and I backed up quickly into the parking meter, which knocked me down once more. **FML**

*

Today, I tried to help an old lady with her groceries. When I asked if she needed a hand, she smiled. When I took one of her bags, she yelled. She was deaf. **FML**

*

Today, I was in the back seat of my friend's car, on the motorway. I looked over to the next lane and was greeted by a van full of adolescent boys waving and making the 'call me' hand gesture. I then happened to look down and realized that my right boob was completely out. **FML**

Today, in a very crowded public toilet at a sporting arena, my six-year-old son looked at the man using the urinal to his right, then turned to address me on his left and exclaimed, 'Daddy, that man's willy is a lot bigger than yours!' The whole room heard and looked immediately at me. **FML**

*

Today, as I was getting restless in my psychology class, I proceeded to stretch out both of my arms into the aisles on either side of me … only to find myself with my teacher's package in my palm. **FML**

Today, I wore a garter belt and fishnet stockings to give my husband a treat. He told me I looked like a joint of pork tied up with string. **FML**

Today, I was pushing my four-year-old on the swing. I did what we call our 'under doggie push': I threw her up in the air, then I ran underneath her before she came back down. I walked away to get my water and she yelled across the park, 'Can we do it doggie-style again?' **FML**

*

Today, I had to play the role of Superman in a production on stage. They had to stuff my underwear because my 'thing' wasn't big enough. **FML**

Today, at work, I was alone in the staffroom when I got a slight pain in my belly. I thought I needed to pass wind, so I tried, since no one else was in there. It wasn't wind. It was diarrhoea. I was wearing a mini-skirt today. **FML**

*

Today, I was working at a supermarket and a very old woman wanted to give me a tip for packing her shopping. She slid a pound coin into my pocket against my thigh, pushed it as deep down as she could get it, then she gave me a smile and a wink. I was groped by a grandma. **FML**

*

Today, I was babysitting an eleven-year-old boy. He decided we should play with guns with velcro tips. I shot him in the crotch accidentally, and the dart stuck on his trousers, wiggling about for a full minute before his dad walked in to find us both staring at his son's crotch, giggling. **FML**

*

Today, I was giving a friend a neck rub, when she started to breathe heavily. I figured she was getting into it, so I started kissing her neck. She then turned around and said, 'Tell my flatmate I'm having an asthma attack.' **FML**

*

Today, I decided to get dressed up for college because it's my birthday. I was heading to class in my heels. Then I went over on my ankle, fell down a muddy hill, pulled a leg muscle and scratched my knees. At least ten people saw it. I was wearing a white skirt. Happy Birthday. **FML**

Today, I yelled at my spouse in front of twenty guests for not coming to blow out his birthday cake candles. Turns out he was in the other room, quietly changing his disabled friend's adult nappy. **FML**

*

Today, my religious girlfriend of eight months finally agreed to have sex with me. She invites me over, and just as we are about to do it, her dad comes home from work three hours early. She says it is a sign from God that we have to wait. **FML**

Today, I took a shower after football practice. When I got out of the shower, I thought no one was home, so I thought it might be fun to walk around the house completely naked. I went downstairs and my mum was eating dinner. Along with twenty members of her book club. **FML**

Today, I was teaching a swimming lesson to six-
and seven-year-old boys and girls. I recently
broke up with my boyfriend, so I haven't been
taking care of my bikini line. While I was
demonstrating a move out of the water, one of the
boys said, 'You have a beard coming out of your
costume!' **FML**

*

Today, I was in the car on a ten-hour road trip
with my family. I fell asleep as soon as we got on
the motorway. When I woke up an hour later, I
realized I'd had a wet dream. I had to sit next to
my grandma with semen all over my thighs and
boxers for the rest of the trip. **FML**

*

Today, I finally mustered the courage to skip out
of my lecture early, only to find that the back door
was locked. As I stood there like an idiot trying to
get it open, all 200 people in my class turned to
laugh. My tutor stared at me. I walked back to my
seat, sat down and took out my notebook. **FML**

*

Today, my mum told my boyfriend all about how
she had to be a parent volunteer when I was at
nursery. Apparently I used to masturbate in class
by rubbing myself against the edges of chairs and
tables. The teacher thought it would be best if my
mum was there to make me stop. **FML**

*

Today, I had a meeting with my super-hot tutor.
When I got to her office, she complimented me
for being early, to which I thoughtlessly replied,
'Oh, I usually come early.' She laughed. **FML**

Today, I unexpectedly got my period at lacrosse practice. Our playing field is a half-mile run away from any toilets so I headed towards the woods with a tampon. Just as I was about to insert the tampon, the entire boys' cross-country team ran by ... laughing. **FML**

*

Today, I went to my new doctor and had to fill in some paperwork. During the questionnaire, she asked if I was sexually active. I said yes. She then asked, 'What do you do?' I told her I normally did vaginal, but would sometimes do anal. She blushed and started to laugh. She was asking my profession. **FML**

***

LIFE'S NOT FAIR

Today, I fell asleep on the train. When I woke up, everybody was staring at me with a strange smile. I'll probably never know what I did. **FML**

Today, my elderly neighbour made puppy eyes at me so that I'd lug her seven bags of groceries up three flights of stairs. Afterwards, very grateful, she took out her purse, handed me a coin, and then told me that maybe that way I could afford to 'get a better haircut next time'. **FML**

Today, I asked my mother if she thought my cat was getting fat. She replied, 'It's not the cat you should worry about.' **FML**

Today, when my husband got home from work, I was standing in the kitchen wearing nothing but stilettos. He asked me to make him a hot chocolate. **FML**

Today, I got back from a six-month deployment overseas. My girlfriend of three years couldn't pick me up from the airport because she had a netball game to go to. **FML**

*

Today, I was napping in my room when my dog started to bark. He does this all the time so I ignored it. This went on for about a half hour. When I went downstairs, I found an open door and an empty TV stand. **FML**

*

Today, I checked Facebook, only to find out that my close cousin is now married. When I looked at the pictures, I saw that my whole family was there – including my sister, mother and father. I was the only one who wasn't invited. **FML**

*

Today, I finally met someone with the same first name as me for the first time ever. I'm twenty years old, he is ninety-seven. **FML**

Today, I began to undress my wife, who was watching TV, and gave her a massage to relax her while she watched her soap. Twenty minutes later, when the programme came to an end, she said, 'I wish you'd let me watch TV in peace!' **FML**

✱

Today, I gave a hand to a charming and sweet old lady to help her cross the road. Once over to the other side, she knocked into the edge of the pavement and I couldn't hold on to her. She screamed, 'You fucking son of a bitch!' at me from the ground. **FML**

✱

Today, I had a horrible day at work, came home early and burst into tears as soon as I was in the door. I curled up on the sofa, still bawling, and my cat came over and jumped up for a cuddle. I gave her a hug and she threw up down my back. **FML**

✱

Today, as I was pressed for time, I opened some tinned food for dinner. When my children were served, they said, 'Mmmm, this is the best meal you've ever cooked for us!' I cook healthy, balanced meals every day. **FML**

✱

Today, I decided to go to my ex-girlfriend's to take her stuff back. We broke up earlier this week after a two-year relationship, and I was hoping she might have realized her mistake and ask me to stay for a bit and talk. I rang the doorbell and her new boyfriend opened the door. **FML**

Today, my boss asked me, 'Can I give you some constructive criticism?' I said yes. He tells me, 'Your work is really shit. You have no talent and I can't figure out why I hired you.' **FML**

*

Today, I was babysitting four rather noisy and rowdy kids. After a two-hour struggle, I finally managed to get them into bed. I then asked them what they wanted before going to sleep, and the eldest replied, 'Can you tell us a story where you die at the end?' **FML**

*

Today, while getting petrol, I began thinking about what a failure my life is, and how badly I've treated people in my past. While deep in thought, I accidentally pulled the petrol nozzle out too far and covered myself with petrol. **FML**

*

Today, I tried to cuddle Simon, my five-year-old son. He wriggled away and said, 'If you need a teddy bear, go and buy one! Or find another Simon!' **FML**

*

Today, my two favourite things in the world are pizza and beer ... and I've just discovered I have coeliac disease and can't have either. **FML**

*

Today, a work colleague announced that she is organizing a party. She says, in front of everyone, that I'm not invited to 'avoid ruining the vibe'. **FML**

Today, I stepped in dog shit, barefoot, in my own bathroom. The dog had been outside for two hours previously and I had watched him shit. Apparently he was saving one up for when he got back in the house. **FML**

Today, I walked into the kitchen and accidentally broke my mother's vase. I said, 'Accidents happen.' She replied, 'Yeah, like your birth.' **FML**

✱

Today, I was talking to my eighty-one-year-old widowed grandmother on the phone, and she told me she was giving up sex for Lent. Not only do I now have a vision of my grandma having sex, but I'm also reminded that she's having more sex than me. **FML**

Today, my boyfriend came to visit me for my birthday. Over dinner, he handed me a blank card that had the words 'I love you' hastily written on it. When the waiter came to take our order, he informed him that we'd be paying separately. Happy Birthday. **FML**

*

Today, my family and I watched the video of my birth. When my mother sees me for the first time, she says, 'God, he's ugly!' **FML**

*

Today, my nineteen-year-old girlfriend dumped me because she thinks I'm immature. I'm thirty. **FML**

*

Today, I decided to give things a go with a guy who has fancied me for three years, based purely on my looks. After getting to know my personality, he decided he no longer fancies me at all. **FML**

*

Today, I picked up my cat, not realizing he was asleep. He went wild. I ended up with several cuts, including one on my wrist. Later, a kid at school saw my wrist and told my teacher, who then told my parents. Now everyone thinks I'm either a liar, an attention seeker or an emo. **FML**

*

Today, my grandmother, who has Alzheimer's and can't usually remember my name, had a sudden moment of clarity and asked me why I'm still not married yet. **FML**

Today, my girlfriend and I broke up. She told me I just wasn't her type, but gave me the phone number of one of her friends. Since all the friends I had met had been pretty hot, I called it later. Her friend was a guy. **FML**

Today, I found out that my assistant is now my manager. **FML**

Today, my sister and I got fitted for bridesmaids' dresses. It was pretty sheer material, so I took off my bright pink thong and left it on the changing room hanger. As I was looking at myself in the mirror, a woman came out of the room holding my thong. She had tried it on. **FML**

✱

Today, I told my mum I was excited as my boobs were getting bigger. She told me that that's what happens when you get fat. **FML**

✱

Today, my little sister and I were reading a book together and, out of nowhere, she said, 'I love you.' My heart melted and I told her that I loved her too. Then she told me that she was talking to her stuffed animal, not me. **FML**

Today, I drove an hour in a rainstorm to see my boyfriend. Thirty minutes and one blow job later, he tells me he's going to meet some friends for dinner in half an hour, then kicks me out of his house. It's still raining. **FML**

Today, I realized that due to my recent loss of appetite, instead of losing weight from my thighs as I had hoped, I've actually been losing weight from my already small breasts. **FML**

*

Today, I got a meat pie for lunch. I bit into it and felt something hard. I spat it out. It was a tooth. I checked my mouth in a panic and discovered, with mixed feelings of relief and horror, that the tooth wasn't mine. **FML**

*

Today, I found out that my girlfriend's computer password is 'i_love_mike'. My name is not Mike. **FML**

*

Today, while surfing Facebook, I noticed that someone in my network had recently shifted his relationship status from undeclared to 'single'. We've been dating exclusively for nine months. **FML**

*

Today, I walked past a girl in the cafeteria and she threw up. Naturally, a crowd was drawn. Her friend asked her what was wrong. She pointed at me and said, 'Get him away from me!' I had never met this girl. **FML**

Today, my boyfriend came round to drop off some underwear that I'd left at his house. Not all of what he brought was mine. **FML**

✱

Today, I had sex with a girl who cried out as she came, 'Forgive me, Lord! Forgive me, Lord!' **FML**

✱

Today, I found out that my teacher writes descriptions next to people's names on the register to remind him who people are. By mistake, the descriptions appeared on the whiteboard. Next to my name it said 'tubby'. **FML**

Today, I walked past a man handing out miniature Bibles. He proceeded to hand me one while commenting, 'Here, you look like you need this.' **FML**

Today, I told the guy I have feelings for that I'm interested in him, and asked how he felt about it. He responded, 'I feel fairly neutral about that.' **FML**

Today, I caught one of my cats humping my huge dog while he was asleep ... I'm sleeping with the door closed from now on. **FML**

Today, my company organized a huge party. I went to work dressed in my best outfit. During the lunch break, my boss said to me, 'You really missed out on something yesterday, it was great fun!' **FML**

✱

Today, I was jerking one off and my cat jumped out of nowhere and dug his claws into my shaft. Attempting to knock him away resulted in three nasty gashes that I now have to explain to my wife. **FML**

✱

Today, my company hired a new guy to help on our project. My boss said that he would shadow me for the whole day so he could learn our system. At the end of the day, my boss fired me and handed my company car keys and laptop to my 'shadow for the day', right in front of me. My mum had to pick me up. **FML**

Today, my boyfriend handcuffed me to my bed in my university halls, naked. Then the fire alarm went off, and my boyfriend couldn't find the key. So he left me, and the Resident Advisor found me. The firemen had to cut the chain. **FML**

*

Today, I took my dog to the vet and she was diagnosed with obesity. The vet then told me that dogs usually imitate their owners' eating and behaviour habits. **FML**

*

Today, the guy I fancy told me he was going to take me out somewhere special, so I called in sick for work. Turns out he had made reservations at the restaurant I work at. **FML**

*

Today, I told my mum I loved her a lot. Her reply? 'Thanks.' **FML**

*

Today, the girl I love and I went to visit my parents for the first time. My father grinned and acknowledged that she was a 'keeper', at which she laughed and said we were 'just friends'. I was going to propose to her next week. **FML**

*

Today, for our eight-month anniversary, my boyfriend bought me a hideous necklace with ugly charms hanging off it. I wore it anyway and got a rash from it on the side of my neck. After seeing the rash, my boyfriend accused me of having a love bite from another guy. He broke up with me. **FML**

Today, my boss asked me to work an extra shift. I said I couldn't because I had a date. He told me I didn't need to lie and to just say no next time. **FML**

*

Today, in basketball practice, my coach was putting us in teams. He points to me and says, 'You, go and babysit my son by the stage.' **FML**

*

Today, I told my dad I was going to get some beauty sleep. He looked at me, laughing, and said, 'See you in a decade.' **FML**

*

Today, my mother decided she wanted the family to go on a special outing. She asked me to drive everyone when she got home from work. Later, I noticed the house was empty. The whole family, including the dog, had left without telling me. They took my car. **FML**

*

Today, I accompanied some friends to sign up for a gym. When we got there, the guy handed me a form, too. I said, 'Oh, I'm not signing up.' He replied, 'Out of all of you, you need it the most.' He then said he was also a nutritionist, and offered a consultation. **FML**

*

Today, my best friend slapped me and called me some colourful names before telling me that she never wanted to talk to me again because I supposedly slept with her boyfriend. Not only am I a virgin, I'm also a lesbian. **FML**

Today, while at work, I sold a ton of eggs to a bunch of kids. We joked around that they were going to bake a giant cake. When I got home, I found out that someone had egged my house. **FML**

*

Today, I woke up happy because I'd met the man of my dreams at a bar. We had shared an amazing night together. I walked around my apartment, wondering where he was. Turns out, he was gone. So was my car. **FML**

Today, when I visited my grandmother at her nursing home, I was looking at the pictures she had up of all the grandkids. All were normal graduation pictures etc., but mine was a cut-out where she had made me skinnier. **FML**

Today, the girl I love told me she was sick of guys. I replied that I happened to be a guy. She laughed and said, 'No, I mean the boyfriend type!' **FML**

*

Today, at a strategy session, my manager displayed a flowchart of his employees. I wasn't included. Apparently, I had been fired. They forgot to tell me. **FML**

Today, I did my work, the work of my colleague who called in sick and the work of my boss, who has no idea what the hell is going on, all at the same time. I didn't get a promotion because I don't work hard enough. **FML**

Today, I went skinny-dipping with my best friend. We were on the beach and it was fairly crowded, but we got in the water near this really secluded area. While we were swimming, I looked up to see a homeless man wearing my clothes, walking away. **FML**

Today, I spent £20 on a spray tan, £30 to have my make-up done, and £50 on a new dress, all for a special date with my boyfriend. It turns out I spent £100 just to get dumped. **FML**

Today, my grandmother called. She greeted me by my mother's name. When I told her it was not my mother, she apologized and corrected herself, but this time she addressed me as my sister. When I told her it was not my sister either, she said, 'Sorry, wrong number,' and hung up. **FML**

*

Today, my boyfriend gave me a gift card for £18 for a local salon. I thought the amount was kind of random, but when I went in I saw that the bikini wax was £18. **FML**

*

Today, I found a note in my locker from a really stunning guy, asking me out. I went up to him with the note in my hand, saying how excited I was to go. He said, 'Oh, *you* got the note?' Then he took it from me and slipped it into the locker next to mine. **FML**

*

Today, I told my parents I really missed them and wanted to come home for the weekend. I haven't seen them in months. They told me that was a bad idea and they couldn't fit me into their schedule. I asked what their plans were. They said they didn't have any yet. **FML**

*

Today, my boyfriend broke up with me. He said I was way too good at sex so I must have lied about not having much experience, and he 'wouldn't be with someone who is hiding something'. WTF? **FML**

Today, my boyfriend and I were in La Senza. I saw a picture of a model and said, 'I wish I looked like that.' He sighed and replied, 'Me too.' **FML**

*

Today, in school, my shoulder was killing me from a tennis injury. I went to the nurse's office and asked, 'Can I have some ice?' They responded with, 'Oh no, what happened to your face?' **FML**

Today, I went for a run and took my shirt off partway through. The next person I saw was a nine-year-old girl playing outside her house. She looked at me and said, 'Eww! That's disgusting!' **FML**

Today, I was just about to orgasm when my girlfriend looked at my clock and said, 'I have to go. *Lost* is on in twenty minutes.' **FML**

*

Today, I went to the hair salon to cut six inches off my hair. When I got there, I decided to get my upper lip waxed for the first time too. When my boyfriend came to pick me up later for our date, I asked him if he noticed anything different about me. The first thing he said was: 'I see you got rid of your moustache.' **FML**

*

Today, I told my mum I loved her, and she asked if I was going to kill myself. **FML**

Today, I came back from university and visited my parents' house. There was a family portrait hung over the mantelpiece, of my parents and two sisters. My mum had always wanted one, but had kept on postponing it. It was dated the day after I left for uni. **FML**

*

Today, I walked downstairs in a new outfit, after dieting for three months and losing just over 20 lbs. My mum took one look at me and said, 'You'd better keep going.' **FML**

*

Today, I had sex with a guy I really like for the first time. I took off my shirt and bra and he said, 'Wow, that's disappointing.' **FML**

*

Today, my boyfriend and I were in his room watching a movie when he started kissing me. Things heated up so we moved over to his bed. He was on top of me when a hand shot down from the top bunk. His brother had been up there the whole time and wanted a high five. So they high-fived. **FML**

*

Today, this guy that I have been in love with for two years asked me into an empty classroom. He handed me a bouquet of flowers and a T-shirt with 'Prom?' on it. I said it was the most adorable thing I had ever seen. He asked if I thought my best friend would like it. **FML**

Today, I just got my car fixed from an accident and drove to a party in a bad thunderstorm. When the power went out, everyone decided to watch the storm from the front windows. Someone mentioned how it would be funny if the tree fell on my car with everyone watching. Twenty seconds later, it did. **FML**

Today, at a festival, a bunch of guys accidentally knocked down a Portaloo while moshing. I was inside that Portaloo. **FML**

Today, after football practice, I was walking to the car with my dad. My teammates waved and said, 'Bye, Pothead!' They call me that because they think my head is shaped like a pot. Of course, my dad didn't believe me. I'm grounded now because I have an abnormally shaped head. I've never smoked pot. **FML**

Today, I was questioned about a request for a restraining order filed against me by an old woman. According to the report, she's seen me 'walking near her house and waving at her' for the last two months. I've been her next-door neighbour for a year and a half. **FML**

✱

Today, I had sex with my girlfriend. Being the stud that I am, after a short time I turned to her and said, 'You think you're ready for round two?' She replied, 'No, but I think I'm ready for the rest of round one.' **FML**

✱

Today, three days before my wedding day, I found out that my fiancé is sleeping with one of my bridesmaids. I just cancelled a £125,000 wedding. I would go into more detail, but I have to help my family (who flew in from Poland, California and Massachusetts) book flights back home. **FML**

✱

Today, while driving my kids to school, my son said, 'Why don't you find another place to live, so we can just live with Daddy?' Then my daughter added, 'Yeah, cos we love Daddy.' **FML**

✱

Today, I proposed to my girlfriend, who I'm madly in love with, by having a plane fly over her house with the message 'Marry me, Abby?' After seeing this, she locked herself in her room and cried for four hours, exclaiming that this wasn't how she wanted to be proposed to. I had invited my entire family. **FML**

Today, I got braces. When I got back in the car after having them fitted, my dad looked over at me and then said to my mum, 'Well, at least we don't have to worry about boys for the next two years.' **FML**

*

Today, I went to the gym and worked out with a trainer. While doing arm exercises, he commented on how impressed he was with the size of my triceps. That really boosted my confidence, until he leaned in to feel them and said, 'Oh, it's just fat.' **FML**

*

Today, my lesbian sister enthusiastically showed me her new strap-on. Not only does she get more girls than me, she now has a bigger penis, too. **FML**

*

Today, I was walking through town with my boyfriend of a year and a half. There was a sign outside a jewellery shop that said: 'Engagement Rings – No Interest for Twelve Months.' I said, 'Look, baby! No interest.' He replied, 'That's right … no interest.' **FML**

*

Today, I finally told my best friend, who I've secretly been in love with for two years, that I was in love with her – but at the last second I chickened out and said I was joking. She replied, 'Don't scare me like that. I thought I was going to have to find a new best friend for a second!' **FML**

Today, I was in the bank with my seven-year-old daughter when I saw an old school friend of mine with his wife. I said hello, and he commented on how beautiful my little girl is. I thanked him, and as I turned away, I heard his wife say, 'I guess the father must be the good-looking one.' **FML**

Today, I went for a medical. My nurse was morbidly obese and unattractive. She told me she would go through the tests listed on the sheet. She did everything, including feeling my genitalia. When it was done, I read over the sheet. Genitalia wasn't a test listed. **FML**

Today, I was having phone sex with my boyfriend. About halfway through, he went really quiet and started breathing heavily. I thought he was about to climax ... until I discovered he had fallen asleep. **FML**

*

Today, I was lying with my girlfriend on the couch. I looked at her and said, 'You're so beautiful. How did I ever get you?' She replied, 'I was drunk.' **FML**

*

Today, I went to get my eyebrows waxed. The woman asked me if I wanted 'them all off'. Not fully understanding what she said, I agreed. When she showed me the mirror, she had taken off my whole eyebrow. **FML**

Today, my wife and I drove to the petrol station. She let me out before she pulled up to the pumps because I wanted to buy some things from the shop. I returned to see my wife proudly filling the tank, something she never does. Smiling, she told me that diesel was cheaper than ordinary petrol. We don't own a diesel car. **FML**

*

Today, for our two-year anniversary, I got my girlfriend a very expensive diamond necklace. She got me male enhancement pills. **FML**

*

Today, I drove my two kids to their friends' houses. As I was in my convertible, looking what I thought was my best, I slowed down outside a bar which had cute, twenty-year-old girls out front. My daughter noticed the speed reduction and said, 'Keep driving, Dad, you're fat and Mum left you for a reason.' **FML**

*

Today, my best friend, who I have been secretly in love with forever, was ranting about her ex-girlfriend. Then she said, 'If only you were gay, we'd be perfect for each other.' So I took the chance to tell her I was. She responded, 'Well, I'm still not attracted to you, though.' **FML**

*

Today, I went to visit my grandmother, accidentally leaving my phone at home. When I got back, I had two texts from the guy I fancy, one saying, 'I want to take the most beautiful girl out for dinner – go with me?' and the other saying, 'Fine, fatty, I'll ask someone else.' **FML**

Today, I was picking up my daughter from my ex-husband's house and his new girlfriend was there. I called to my daughter that it was time to leave and she clung to his girlfriend and said, 'Mummy, I don't want to leave.' She wasn't talking to me. **FML**

Today, I was playing musical chairs at a family reunion. It's a well-known fact that I'm competitive and will go to any lengths to get that last chair. It came down to me and Nana. I won. Nana now has a broken hip. **FML**

Today, I was serving a table full of drunk people. They used the candles on the table to set the table on fire. Noticing this, I ran to it and poured a pitcher of water on it. Then other tables complained, saying I was causing a disturbance. I got fired for putting out a fire. **FML**

Today, all of my friends and teachers asked me what was wrong because I looked sad and tired. One kid even said that I looked like 'an abused housewife the day after'. I was fine. It was the first time I'd been to college without wearing any make-up. **FML**

∗

Today, I sent an email to my best friend, telling him that I'm gay. But my computer autocorrected his email address to my mother's, without me realizing. She just responded: 'You filthy faggot.' **FML**

∗

Today, I was walking from my office to the place I had parked my car. As I was about to round the corner, I was forced to dive out of the way of a speeding car. As I looked up, I noticed that it was my car. **FML**

Today, I was at a club. I was dancing with this guy when I felt something move in his pants. I stood up and stepped away. He said, 'Don't flatter yourself, it was my phone.' **FML**

Today, I arrived at work, only to be arrested and accused of stealing over £8,000. Five hours later, at the police station, the discovery was made that the actual thief had an employee ID that was one digit different from mine. He works at another location over 100 miles away. **FML**

Today, I emailed the guy I like to ask him out for a coffee. He declined by telling me he never drinks coffee. We first met at Starbucks. **FML**

*

Today, my boss had to leave the house for a little while. She asked me to take any messages she got. I answered the phone and the lady calling said she was returning my boss's call about the opening for a nanny position. I am the current nanny. I found out I am being fired from the new nanny. **FML**

*

Today, my boss told me that I was hired because of how much I reminded him of his daughter. Taking this as a compliment, I mentioned it to a colleague I was trying to impress. I later found out that my boss's daughter is both clinically obese and mentally challenged. **FML**

*

Today, I was pulled over because I looked like a suspect in a robbery. While I was being searched, the police radio went off and the person on the other end said, 'Possible suspect: five foot five, thin.' The officer stopped his search right then and murmured, 'Too short and fat,' and walked straight back to his car. **FML**

*

Today, my brother's new girlfriend, who is blind, asked to feel my face so she could tell what I looked like. She said I was 'unique'. A blind chick just told me I was ugly. **FML**

Today, I was walking to school and decided to be a good citizen, so I picked up a beer can that had been discarded on the pavement, thinking I'd throw it away at the next dustbin. There were none en route. Arriving at school with the can still in my hand, I was suspended for 'trying to rebel'. My parents later grounded me for getting suspended. **FML**

*

Today, I was shopping with my friends and a man asked me if I would be in one of his commercials. I obviously said yes without thinking twice. I then found out that he wanted me to be the 'before' picture for an acne-control moisturizer. **FML**

Today, it was my girlfriend's birthday. I told her that I was going away on business and could not be there. When I showed up at her house to surprise her, with presents and a cake, she opened the door in her underwear, beside a man in his boxers. She was surprised. **FML**

Today, I spotted a girl I hooked up with last weekend on the computer in the library. I noticed she was looking at my Facebook page and got excited. Then I heard her say to her friend, 'His was the smallest penis I have ever seen.' **FML**

Today, at the dinner table, my parents were talking to my younger sister about her new boyfriend and how they should be taking things slowly. My sister then pointed out that that's not what I do. My dad said, 'Believe me, I know – your sister's easier to get into than a packet of crisps.' **FML**

Today, I finally plucked up the courage to tell my best friend that I've had a crush on him since primary school. I sent him a text. His response: 'Yeah, I know. I've tried kind of ignoring it.' **FML**

*

Today, my first girlfriend of over three years left me for another guy. She said she's looking for someone who can financially provide for her in the future. He works in a T-Mobile shop. I'm going to medical school. **FML**

*

Today, I told my boyfriend, 'We need to talk.' He said, 'I know.' So we met after school, and he said he was OK with me breaking up with him, that he wasn't that into me either. He said all that before I could tell him that my parents wanted to meet him. **FML**

Today, I was at a strip club. A stripper came over to me, grabbed my tits and said I had bigger ones than her. I'm a guy. **FML**

∗

Today, after work, I went to the car park to get my car to go home. I found my car doors heavily scratched and all my tyres slashed, with a note on my windscreen. The note read: 'Fuck you, Jackson. Don't fuck with me.' I'm Richard. Jackson is my colleague. **FML**

∗

Today, I found the password to my boyfriend's chat account and logged in. I was listed in the 'booty call' category. **FML**

∗∗∗

MORTIFYING MOMENTS

Today, I wanted to see if the frying pan was hot. I no longer have fingerprints. **FML**

Today, I was hitting on a girl who was getting ready to walk into the same class as me. We were waiting outside the room, and I told her that I'd heard the tutor for the course was a total bitch. We walked into the room. I sat down at a desk. She stood behind the podium. **FML**

*

Today, while shaving, I cut myself – with the blade protector. **FML**

*

Today, I was on a date with my new boyfriend. I acted very flirty and laughed very loudly to show him how funny he was. I laughed so loudly that I farted. **FML**

*

Today, I asked a guy if I could have his phone number, having had a tremendously hot time with him after meeting that same night. He replied, 'What for?' **FML**

Today, in one of the corridors at college, I was pretending to have passionate sex with one of my teachers to make my friends laugh; she passed just behind me, reminding me at the same time of the date of my next exam. She will be marking me. **FML**

∗

Today, I told myself, 'Go on, you big geek, go outside, get some sun, get away from your computer, go for a walk.' I finally mustered the courage to leave my house – without my keys. I've been in an Internet cafe for four hours. **FML**

∗

Today, my mistress called my wife. **FML**

Today, a young girl asked me to buy some of her home-made cookies for charity. She looked nice, so I bought five boxes from her. She took the money and went home with her mum. I opened the boxes when I got home and realized that they just had rocks in them. I got totally scammed. **FML**

Today, feeling romantic and overwhelmed with love, I told my fiancée, 'I don't know what I'd do without you ...' She replied, 'Well, you'd wank.' **FML**

✳

Today, we were walking around and smoking a bit of spliff. We saw a place to sit down in this little car park. The police came over and busted us. Turns out we were in the car park of the police station. **FML**

Today, my son looked out of the window and said, 'What's that piece of shit doing in our driveway?' It was the new car we were hoping to surprise him with on his birthday. **FML**

Today, my girlfriend and I went to a nightclub. When the song 'Single Ladies' by Beyoncé came on, the DJ took the mike and shouted, 'Single ladies, raise your hands!' My girlfriend raised her hand. **FML**

✳

Today, my husband came home from work angry. He started yelling about how much he hates the neighbours' kids and that he never wants to have children. I was going to tell him I'm pregnant tonight. **FML**

Today, I had to go to my son's school for career day. I explained what a banker does and then I asked if anyone had a question. One boy raised his hand and asked, 'When are the cool parents coming in?' **FML**

*

Today, I lied and said I was late for work because my car's tyre was flat. Two hours later, some of my friends came in and said, 'We should do brunch every Saturday, like this morning – it was great!' in front of my manager. **FML**

*

Today, I was driving at night and saw a small animal run across the road. I slammed on my brakes and someone crashed into the back of me. The animal turned out to be a plastic bag. **FML**

*

Today, I went shopping with this girl I like while my girlfriend was busy. We ended up in the supermarket, buying ingredients to make dinner together, when I ran into my girlfriend's parents. **FML**

*

Today, after I'd been looking for my phone for two days, I realized that the vegetable compartment in the fridge was vibrating. **FML**

*

Today, wanting a change from my usual pizza and Coke menu, I decided to cook. After spending an hour and a half making a chilli, I sprinkled a bit of salt over it. The top came off the salt. **FML**

Today, when I was with my boyfriend, I walked ahead of him 'catwalk style', turned around and asked, 'Do you think I can model?' He blurted out, 'Yes ... for a plus-size clothing line.' **FML**

*

Today, I decided to quit smoking and put on a nicotine patch. I then decided to have one last cigarette ... and ended up at the doctors with nicotine poisoning. **FML**

*

Today, I won £500 on a scratch card and tried to give the man sitting next to me a high five. He had no hands. **FML**

*

Today, I was masturbating on the bottom of my bunk beds. After I'd finished, I tried to get up to clean myself, but hit my head on the metal panel of the upper bunk and passed out. My parents came home and found me passed out, naked, holding a porn mag. **FML**

*

Today, I promised my best friend I wouldn't let her get off with any guys since she caught an STD a few weeks ago. After we knocked a few back, she led about thirty people in a chant of 'cock block' after I wouldn't let her go home with some random bloke. **FML**

*

Today, I made fun of my friend when she tripped over the kerb. I said loudly, 'Ha, ha, you can't even walk.' I then noticed the man in the wheelchair a few feet ahead of us. **FML**

Today, my husband of nine years announced he was gay. He insinuated that he was only able to achieve erections because I looked like a man. **FML**

*

Today, I saw a homeless man asking for money. Not wanting to give him any to spend on booze, I decided to buy him a full Big Mac meal from McDonald's. When I went to hand it to him, he quickly waved his hand, saying, 'Thanks, but I'm a vegetarian.' **FML**

*

Today, I was finally able to get to know a girl who I've been eyeing up for months. We had a nice conversation. We discovered that we live in the same area, and so we talked about that. I told her that the little restaurant under my apartment was really disgusting. Her parents own it. **FML**

*

Today, I was my friend's wedding photographer. I took stupid pictures all day long. The moment the bride entered the church, my battery died. **FML**

*

Today, I went to surprise my boyfriend in the shower. I opened the door and there was a giant turd in the toilet. I pretended I was looking for my hairbrush. **FML**

*

Today, my overprotective mum decided to do an ultraviolet-light test on my room to make sure I wasn't doing the naughty. The bed was clean; my face wasn't. **FML**

Today, on the toilet, I decided that I was bored and began to paint my nails. I had to wait at least thirty minutes to wipe. **FML**

*

Today, I was having sex with my girlfriend. As I pulled out to finish, I slipped and ended up punching her in the stomach. I came while she was writhing in pain. **FML**

*

Today, I decided to make a Pop Tart. It fell through the grate in the toaster and burst into flames. After five minutes of me fanning the smoke away from the smoke detector, it was still going off. Now my entire building is outside in a snowstorm. **FML**

*

Today, I was at a bar in Canada and was really hitting it off with a girl. She asked how big my cock was and I told her, in inches. They use centimetres. **FML**

Today, I was going down on a girl. When I looked up, she was texting. **FML**

Today, a toddler's ball rolled over to me in the park. I playfully pitched it to him as his parents watched from afar. The ball hit him in the face. **FML**

*

Today, I thought I was giving a woman the orgasm of a lifetime until I realized that she was telling me to stop pulling her hair. **FML**

Today, I broke up with my boyfriend. I called him two minutes after I'd left, and he had already fallen asleep. **FML**

Today, I was looking at porn on my laptop when my mum came into my room to talk to me. After she finished what she was saying, she paused and said, 'You know I can see the reflection of your computer screen in your glasses.' **FML**

*

Today, my girlfriend snuck up behind me to cover my eyes and play 'Guess Who?' The second her hands touched my face, I instinctively grabbed her, twisted her wrists, and kneed her to the floor. **FML**

*

Today, I slept with this new guy for the first time. After sex, he said that doggie style was fun – it put him in mind of what it would be like to rape a girl. **FML**

Today, my girlfriend asked if her friend Alex
could join us for a threesome. As a horny bloke,
how could I say no? Turns out, Alex is also a
guy's name. **FML**

✱

Today, I decided to get in shape. I went to buy
some weights. I couldn't take them home – the
box was too heavy. **FML**

✱

Today, after a night out, I got into my building's
lift with a Chinese man who was carrying a plastic
bag. Excited, I asked, 'Ooh, are you still
delivering?' His response: 'I live here.' **FML**

✱

Today, I had a sexy dream, woke up and started
to masturbate quite vigorously. When I finished, I
hopped off the top bunk, naked, to see my
brother and his girlfriend lying in the bottom
bunk, awake. **FML**

✱

Today, I was driving and stopped behind another
car. They didn't move for about a minute. I got
out of my car, yelling at the person. It was an old
woman. She wasn't breathing. **FML**

✱

Today, I spent almost my entire English class
turned on, thinking that the hot girl next to me
was playing footsie with me. That is, until she
stood up and I realized I had been rubbing my
foot on her backpack. **FML**

Today, I noticed a prospective employer I had been networking with had changed her last name on her email signature. I wished the acquaintance congratulations on her new marriage. Her divorce was finalized this week. **FML**

✱

Today, my entire family sat down in the living room to watch the video I recorded of my sister's graduation. I never hit record. **FML**

Today, at lunchtime, I tried hallucinogenic mushrooms for the first time with my friend. Little did I know, they last for around six hours, and I had a class at three, when I had to give a presentation in front of thirty people. **FML**

Today, I went on a first date with an Egyptian/Cuban girl. I asked her what language she was brought up speaking. She said that her mum spoke to her in Spanish, but that she only ever replied in English. I said, 'Oh, kinda like Chewbacca and Han Solo?' **FML**

✱

Today, I was taking the lift down, which was full of people. It stopped on the first floor and before the doors opened, I said, 'What arsehole can't take the steps from the first floor?' A kid in a wheelchair got in. **FML**

Today, I asked my boss for a pay rise. He responded with, 'Who the hell are you?' **FML**

*

Today, I cut myself on a first-aid box, while trying to get a plaster out for another cut. **FML**

*

Today, I changed the C on my school report into a B so I wouldn't get in trouble with my parents. I spent the entire day perfecting the B's positioning and cut exactly around the edges of the size ten font (slicing my finger in the process). I was grounded for getting a B. **FML**

*

Today, while alone in the communal showers in the football changing room, I jokingly started to swing my penis around. Two minutes later, the rest of the team hops into the shower. Thirty dudes, one self-induced boner. **FML**

*

Today, I told the man I'm sleeping with that I thought my sister was prettier than me. His response: 'Not significantly.' **FML**

Today, I woke up next to my girlfriend. When she asked me to pick up her thong from behind my bed, I realized there were two. I didn't pick up hers. **FML**

Today, I was doing a PowerPoint presentation to the management committee. Outlook Express was still open, and right in the middle of the presentation, a window popped up notifying me of a new message. The subject line read: 'RE: your job application for the post of Marketing Manager.' **FML**

Today, after taking a shower, I decided to weigh myself. I peered down. I couldn't see the scales. **FML**

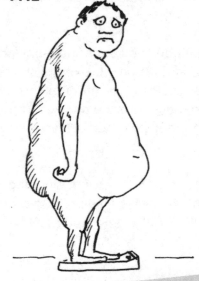

Today, my husband invited his new boss and his wife over for dinner. During the meal, I tasted the wine, apologized for its bad quality and, somewhat annoyed, announced, 'Don't drink that, I'll go and look for another bottle.' Our guests had brought the wine. **FML**

Today, in front of a hospital, I noticed that an old lady was having trouble lighting her cigarette due to her Parkinson's. I helped her to light it up and she then started chatting with me and told me she had lung cancer. **FML**

*

Today, I found out that when I masturbate at night while watching Internet porn, I cast a huge shadow on the curtain and the entire street is able to see it. **FML**

Today, I was on a transatlantic flight with earplugs in my ears. The steward walked past with a plastic bag. I threw my litter into it and didn't immediately understand why he said, 'Very funny, sir.' It wasn't for rubbish – he was collecting for UNICEF. **FML**

Today, I went to fill up my car. Five hundred feet before the petrol station, I saw a motorcycle gang in my rear-view mirror. I slowed down and pulled over to let them pass. They were going to fill up too. Thirty-five motorcycles and two petrol pumps. **FML**

*

Today, I was walking my son to school. After scolding him for not looking where he was going, I grabbed his hand and pulled him closer to me, and I walked him right into a lamp post. **FML**

Today, I met a guy who said he thinks he's in love with my sister. As a joke, I told him that my sister cheats on everyone. I get home to find my sister crying, because someone told her boyfriend that she's cheating on him. **FML**

*

Today, on a crowded train, a gorgeous guy called me over and told me to stand next to him because there were less people there. We started talking, but he left before I could get his number. When I was about to tell my friends about him, I realized that he'd stolen my phone. **FML**

Today, I was helping to supervise a five-year-old's birthday party on an inflatable obstacle course. I was playing hide-and-seek with the kids. I saw the birthday boy, crept around the corner and yelled, 'Found you!' He peed his pants in front of everyone. **FML**

Today, I closed out of a video chat with my boyfriend to take a shit. I took my computer with me to check my email. It took me five minutes to realize I was still on video chat. **FML**

*

Today, I spent three minutes struggling to uncork a wine bottle for one of my tables – only to have them point out to me that the bottle had a screw top. **FML**

Today, I saw my male boss holding a purse. Just to be a smart-arse, I made fun of him as if the purse was his. It was. **FML**

*

Today, I was pulled over for speeding in a 30-mph zone. As the cop was walking towards my car, I flicked my cigarette butt out of my window. He wrote me two tickets instead of one. **FML**

*

Today, I walked past my flatmate and his girlfriend while they were hugging. I asked, 'What's up, lovebirds?' They were in the middle of breaking up. **FML**

*

Today, I drank a ton of beer for my twenty-fifth birthday. My friends love to watch me open beer bottles with my teeth. I chipped both of my front teeth doing this. Twenty-five is when I'm no longer covered by my parents' dental insurance. **FML**

*

Today, I lost £200 while playing poker wearing my new shades. Turns out, you can see the cards in the reflection. **FML**

*

Today, I was at the airport, about to listen to Disney's *Camp Rock* soundtrack on my iPhone. I pressed play, only to realize a minute later that my headphones weren't plugged in all the way. Everyone sitting near me heard Joe Jonas's voice. I am forty years old. **FML**

Today, I saw my friend across campus and decided that I wanted to play a trick on her and scare her from behind. Turns out, I scared a complete stranger with really bad panic-induced asthma. **FML**

*

Today, I studied for 13.5 hours completely outlining a book for history. Thirty minutes before the test, I realized it was the wrong book. **FML**

Today, my five-year-old nephew showed me green Martians he had made with his new Play-Doh set. I smiled and said, 'Wow! Now, how about some blue Martians?' He looked at me and replied, 'How about some blue shut the fuck up?' **FML**

Today, I was doing a striptease for my husband. He asked me to stop. **FML**

*

Today, I was secretly listening to a voicemail from my mum in my maths class when I accidentally hit the speakerphone button. My whole class now knows I have a gynaecologist appointment at 9.45 on 11 March. **FML**

Today, I went to a party with the boy I'm interested in. It was the first time I'd met his friends. Turns out he and all his mates are hard-core Christians who don't drink and are celibate. **FML**

Today, I saw an elderly man fall over, so I jumped off my bike to help. As I assisted him across the road, the traffic lights turned green. At that point, I noticed my phone had fallen out of my pocket. It was run over by several cars. I then watched across a six-lane street as someone stole my bike. **FML**

✱

Today, one of my closest friends and I got into a fight. She ended the conversation with, 'My grandma just had a stroke. Bye.' I didn't believe her so I replied, 'That's great! Bye.' Her grandma is in a critical condition. **FML**

Today, in class, my friend played a joke on me by pulling my seat out from under me when I was about to sit down. I fell and everybody laughed at me. During the next class, I did the same thing to him. He broke his arm. He is the star of the basketball team. Nobody laughed. **FML**

*

Today, I drunk-dialled my mum and told her I was so high and drunk that I thought the KGB was coming after me. When I woke up this morning, my mum told me that she is no longer paying for university. **FML**

*

Today, I called the florist and ordered a flower arrangement for my grandma, who I was told was sick. I didn't know what to get her, so I told them just to send her something nice. I later got a call from my mum, calling me an inconsiderate bastard. They sent my grandma forget-me-nots. She has Alzheimer's. **FML**

*

Today, in a rush, I went to the supermarket to buy some condoms. When I looked at the cashier, I realized it was my girlfriend's father. Nervous and hoping to reassure him, I stuttered, 'Don't worry, I'm not using these with Kim.' That didn't help. **FML**

*

Today, I sent out a note to 300 friends saying that I'm having a birthday party in a couple of weeks. I asked them please to RSVP if they were interested in going. Two people answered. They can't make it. **FML**

Today, I decided to try this new cardio-workout video. As I was enthusiastically bouncing around my room, I heard something behind me. There were three adolescent boys outside my window, watching. **FML**

*

Today, I visited my brother in jail for the first time. I didn't know what to say, so I blurted out, 'Having fun?' **FML**

Today, after class, I was chatting with my teacher, a really cool and stylish old black guy. I tell him he reminds me of one of those soul dudes from those seventies movies, right down to the 'pimp walk'. He tells me he walks that way because he was beaten for drinking out of the wrong fountain as a kid. **FML**

Today, I was over at my boyfriend's house and I heard a strange sound. I laughed and said, 'It sounds like a dog throwing up!' He listened for a second and said, 'That's my mum crying downstairs.' **FML**

*

Today, I asked a very cute fireman for his number 'just in case I needed him to come to my rescue'. He told me, 'Yeah, sure!' and scribbled it down. After he walked away, I read his note: '999.' **FML**

Today, I was at work, about to go to lunch. There were some Girl Guides outside selling cakes. I told my manager that I would be using a different exit, and when he asked why, I told him that Girl Guides really annoy the crap out of me. The Girl Guides outside were his daughters. **FML**

*

Today, I was at the gym, working out for the first time in a while. A really attractive girl there kept shooting me glances. I asked for her number and she responded by saying, 'If you can lift the same weight as me.' I couldn't. **FML**

*

Today, I was the teaching assistant for a history lesson and the class was taking a test. About halfway through, I noticed one kid had a small piece of paper in his hand. I ran up the row, grabbed his test and ripped it into four pieces. Then I looked at the note: 'I believe in you – Mum x.' **FML**

*

Today, an amber light turned red as I was approaching it. I was about to go through but saw a cop, panicked, and slammed on the brakes. I ended up in the middle of the road and had to reverse. Soon the lights turned green, and I set off. My car was still in reverse. **FML**

*

Today, I saw my ex-girlfriend across the street. I was walking with a girl I'd been hanging out with for a while and I wanted to make my ex-girlfriend jealous. I kissed the girl and she smacked me. I got a 'ha, ha!' text from my ex. **FML**

Today, I babysat a five-year-old girl. She ran up to me, threw her arms around my waist and said, 'Yummy! I'm going to eat you!' with her face in my crotch. I said sarcastically under my breath, 'Finally, some action!' I turned around to find her dad staring at me, having heard. **FML**

*

Today, I was babysitting my colleague's son. He was eating jelly and spilt it on his top, so I pulled off his pyjamas and went to his room to grab a new pair. I heard a thump and ran to find him out cold on the floor. His parents walked in on me trying to wake up their naked three-year-old. **FML**

Today, during my choral concert, I was helping to turn the pages for the pianist, who was accompanying the singers. In the middle of a song, one of the pages slipped and fell into his crotch. In a panic, I frantically reached to grab the music. I grabbed something. It wasn't the music. **FML**

Today, I was walking along the street when a man pointed a camera at me. I decided to be bitchy about it and said, 'Did I say you could take a picture?' He replied, 'No, but you can get the fuck out of the way so I can take one of my wife and kids.' I turned around. They were right behind me. **FML**

Today, I buried my girlfriend's recently deceased cat. Later, she asked to see the grave and came back inside crying. I didn't bury it completely. Its two back legs were poking out of the dirt. **FML**

Today, my parents left for work before I had to leave for school and I decided to bunk off. I stayed by the phone so that when the school called, I could pose as my parent and excuse my absence. The phone rang and I picked up. It was my mum, calling to leave my dad a message on the machine. **FML**

*

Today, a guy who I've been on five dates with called me for the first time in two weeks. The first thing I said was: 'Don't expect me to go out with you again after going AWOL on me.' Then he told me his mum had died. **FML**

Today, I went to the movies with some girlfriends. The guy behind us was making these pervy, heavy breathing noises, so we threw some popcorn at him. When the lights came up, we saw he was in a wheelchair – with a breathing tube sticking out of his neck. **FML**

✱

Today, I took my girlfriend to a very nice restaurant. I thought it would be a good place to pop the question. I gave the ring to the waiter and asked him to put it on her dessert plate. When she saw it, she picked it up, put it down and said, 'No.' Then she ate the dessert. **FML**

✱

Today, I was walking down the street and saw a £20 note on the ground. I thought it had fallen out of the pocket of the man in front of me, so I decided to do the right thing and asked him if he'd dropped it. He said yes and took it. I later realized the £20 was mine. **FML**

✱

Today, I was singing Alicia Keys in the shower and hitting the insanely high notes. My father ran into the bathroom and threw open the shower door, screaming. He thought I was wailing in pain. **FML**

✱

Today, I had to run to catch my train, so I didn't get the chance to buy a ticket. When the conductor was in sight, I saw he was a young man and I opened my top a little in the hope of not having to pay a fine. When I told him I hadn't bought a ticket, he said, 'Close your top, I'm gay.' **FML**

Today, I got my first tattoo. It was a surprise for my fiancé: our names together over a heart. I went home, but before I could show him, he said we had to have a 'talk'. Now my ex's name is tattooed on my back. Plus, I'm allergic to the ink. **FML**

*

Today, I walked into my house to find everyone sitting around the table looking sad. I thought it would be a good time to crack a joke and said, 'What's wrong? Grandma finally died?' She had. **FML**

Today, my mother told me she didn't want my girlfriend spending the night anymore. I asked why. She said she'd heard us doing the nasty the night before. I denied it, hoping I could call her bluff. She paused for a moment and then proceeded to moan exactly like my girlfriend. **FML**

Today, I went on a walk with the guy I like. He held my hand, so I decided to tell him that I had feelings for him. He said that he had feelings for me too. I smiled and leaned in to kiss him. He put his hand on my face and pushed it away, saying, 'Until your acne clears, we are not together.' **FML**

Today, we watched a movie in class. Afterwards, the tutor asked us what we thought. I raised my hand and said it was pretentious, dull and a really poor example of film-making. It was the movie he spent five years writing and directing. **FML**

*

Today, I saw two lovely ladies leave my neighbour's house, and a couple of minutes later he walked out. I made the international male 'Did you fuck her/them?' hand gesture – a horizontal fist pump. They were his daughters. **FML**

*

Today, I was babysitting a seven-year-old girl and we were eating chocolate-covered nuts. She kept on chewing the nuts, and wondered aloud where the chocolate was. I told her that to taste the chocolate, you had to suck on the treats. The first thing she told her parents when they got home was: 'I learned how to suck nuts!' **FML**

Today, a guy informed me that the cute, really tiny leather bracelet with little silver hearts and several snaps that I'd found in a shop is a cock ring. I'm a girl. **FML**

Today, I woke up at my grandparents' house. Still half asleep, I went to brush my teeth. Mid-brush, my mouth started going numb. I inspected the toothpaste. It was my grandpa's anti-itch anal cream. **FML**

Today, my best friend resolved things with her boyfriend after he admitted to cheating. I felt really guilty because last month I had drunkenly slept with him. She said to me, 'I felt better when he told me that the girl was extremely ugly and bad in bed.' **FML**

*

Today, the kids I teach informed me that I had spelled my name incorrectly on the board. I looked at it and assured them that I had spelled it correctly. I'm twenty-two and a graduate student, they're six and mentally challenged. Guess who was right? **FML**

Today, I bought a parakeet for my kids. When I got home and presented it to them, they wanted to let him fly around inside. We went around the house making sure all the windows and doors were shut. I forgot the ceiling fan. **FML**

Today, I interviewed for a full scholarship to college. In the interview, I said that I was excited about the new head because I think she'll be able to make improvements and bring the college back to where it used to be. Afterwards, I learned that my interviewer was the former head. **FML**

Today, my family and I were at a restaurant. We're Swedish and love talking about other people in our language because no one else ever understands. I decided to comment on how ugly the girl at the next table was. She turned around and said, '*Dra åt helvete*.' That's Swedish for 'Go to hell'. **FML**

Today, I went over to my uncle's house for dinner and my stomach was really hurting, so I went to the bathroom. I noticed there were two toilets. I sat in the nicer one and proceeded to take a huge dump. Turns out, I chose the brand-new toilet. It hadn't been connected yet. **FML**

*

Today, I went to get my mid-term essay grade, thinking I couldn't have got lower than a B. I got an F. He wrote: 'Best essay I read, would've been an A if it was the right topic.' I wrote on the Industrial Revolution, instead of the Scientific Revolution. **FML**

Today, I was eating lunch naked at home, while watching porn on the big screen. I heard the garage door opening, meaning my flatmate was coming home. In my haste to get dressed, I fell off the bar stool I was sitting on and knocked myself out. I woke up naked with lettuce all over me. **FML**

∗

Today, I was talking to my grandmother, who was lying down on the couch under a blanket watching TV. As I was leaving, I said, 'See you later, Nana,' and patted her on the shoulder. Her shoulder was soft, and moved more than I expected. It was her boob. I felt up my grandmother. **FML**

Today, I went to my friend's house, while his parents were out, to smoke weed. Forty-five minutes into smoking, his parents called to say they'd be home in five minutes. We sprayed the house with Febreze to mask the smell. We were high and in a rush. It was bug spray. **FML**

Today, my mum was helping me unpack from university. She opened a box and took out some anal beads I got as a joke gift. She proceeded to ask, 'What are these?' I answered, 'They're for massaging your back.' She then insisted I show her. I massaged my mother with anal beads. **FML**

Today, I woke up to find my car broken into. I was upset about not hearing my car alarm go off, when I suddenly realized that I had, in the middle of the night. I'd woken up, cursed the idiot who had set off their alarm, put a pillow over my head, and fallen back to sleep. **FML**

*

Today, my friends and I were drinking Boba, a type of East Asian tea. On the side of the cup, it said: 'Please drink carefully to avoid choking on the Boba.' I started to laugh at the ridiculousness of the label, and proceeded to choke on the Boba in a coughing fit. **FML**

*

Today, when I was shaving, I wanted to see what I looked like with a Hitler moustache, so I just left that part and figured I'd shave it off later. I then messed around in my room for a while and forgot all about it. I ran into my girlfriend's parents later that day. **FML**

Today, I babysat three-year-old twins. They have a huge whiteboard hanging between their beds. After they fell asleep, I was bored and drew a very detailed and large picture of a penis on it. When I went to erase it, I realized I'd done it in indelible ink. **FML**

Today, my child told me, 'Mummy, sometimes my willy goes up like a stick.' I said, 'Well, that's normal and OK.' Then I asked when it does that. He replied, 'Well, sometimes when watching *Scooby-Doo* and Shaggy comes out dressed in lady clothes.' **FML**

*

Today, I met a really nice couple at a bar. We talked and the conversation eventually drifted towards online dating. I casually commented that meeting through the Internet was sad and pathetic. They met on MySpace. **FML**

*

Today, I was giving my boyfriend a love bite when I felt something squirt into my mouth. I'd popped a pimple on his neck into my mouth. **FML**

*

Today, I found an old dress lying around the house. I decided to dye it green to wear on St Patrick's Day. It was my grandmother's wedding dress that my sister was planning to wear for her wedding. **FML**

*

Today, my mother called me and told me that she was in hospital. This wasn't a surprise because she goes to hospital for the smallest things. So I was a smart-arse and asked, 'What now? You finally have lung cancer from all those cigarettes?' She does. **FML**

OUT OF
LUCK

Today, I waited two hours for my turn in hospital. I was sitting next to an old lady with Alzheimer's, who asked me forty-three times if I wanted a biscuit. **FML**

Today, I was the only one in a lift when an attractive girl came in, talking on her phone. She told her friend, 'I have to go, there's a hot guy in this lift.' Before I could even react, she turned to me and said, 'Sorry for lying, I really wanted to get off the phone.' **FML**

Today, my boyfriend of four years proposed to me. I wasn't expecting anything too romantic, but I would have liked something more than an email from Facebook requesting my confirmation that we were engaged. **FML**

*

Today, while walking in the forest, I hit my foot against a half-buried metal object. I dug into the ground and it was a beautiful box, heavy enough not to be empty. I imagined myself rich with gold coins. It was the corpse of a dead cat. **FML**

*

Today, I was making a smoothie. I put all the ingredients in. I pushed the 'on' button. It was still on when I went to plug it in ... with no lid. **FML**

Today, I woke up hungover and thirsty. I found a glass of water next to the sink, filled it up with more water, chugged it and went back to bed. I woke up an hour later to my best friend telling me she thought she had lost her contacts. They were in a glass next to the sink. I ate her contacts. **FML**

Today, I was rejected from my first choice of university. My dad has been a professor there for thirty years, and is on the board of admissions. **FML**

Today, I was at a restaurant with a girl I like, and as I was getting my wallet out, I dropped a condom. She didn't see anything, and I waited to pick it up in case I drew attention to it. Then the waiter walked past, picked it up and held it out to me with a huge grin. **FML**

Today, we got our school yearbooks. I opened to my profile, to see that they had misspelled my first name, which is James. They had written Lames. **FML**

Today, and for the last eight months, my upstairs neighbours have been making a tremendous noise. I finally decided to go up to complain: 'The amount of noise you make is unbelievable! It sounds like you're riding tractors up here!' The woman replied, 'My husband is paraplegic.' **FML**

✻

Today, I bought a new, fancy, very expensive electric razor. I tried it, and washed it. I started to shake it dry. It was pretty slippery, and it exploded on the floor of my bathroom. **FML**

✻

Today, I came home to find a puppy in my back garden. Thinking it was lost or a stray, I took it to the RSPCA. My boyfriend came home and asked me if I had seen my present: the puppy. We went back to get it, but it had already been adopted. **FML**

Today, I suggested that my mother download Skype so we could video chat while I'm studying abroad over the summer. After I had explained how it worked and that it was free, she said, 'Well ... you'll only be gone for a few months. It's not really worth it.' **FML**

✱

Today, before a big formal banquet, I went on a sunbed because I wanted to look good in my cocktail dress. Afterwards, I realized that I had left my socks on. **FML**

✱

Today, I had the cops called on me because I accidentally texted 'I'm going to kill you and use your head as an ornament' to my ex-fiancée instead of my best friend. He got a better grade on an exam than me. I now have a court date. **FML**

✱

Today, I was in a lift with my girlfriend when it got stuck between floors. Being supportive, I went to hug her and tell her we'd be OK. Today, I also learned that my girlfriend is claustrophobic and her predominant reaction is to vomit. All over me. We were stuck for two hours. **FML**

✱

Today, I was at the airport in India, where the men and women are searched separately. The guy welcoming us pointed me towards the women's area. It took me fifteen minutes to explain that I'm a guy. **FML**

Today, I was cutting a bagel, only to slice the back of my hand with the knife. As I grabbed paper towels to clean up the blood, I noticed that the bagel was pre-sliced. **FML**

*

Today, my wife, in her pristine wedding dress, had her period during the ceremony. How did I find out? The same way everyone else did. **FML**

*

Today, I drank a beer that I thought was mine. It wasn't. Someone had put out their cigarette in it. **FML**

*

Today, I tried to be smart and show the guys in the office that I can turn on my home webcam remotely. So we all found out together that my wife is cheating on me. **FML**

Today, I was stuck for forty minutes in a traffic jam after a car overturned. When the traffic finally began to move, my car wouldn't start, since I'd left the headlights on and been listening to the radio. I was in the middle lane of the motorway. **FML**

Today, I'm sick. I had the flu jab for the first time ever this year – and for the first time in my life, I have flu. **FML**

Today, I was told that my mum and her new husband have named my newborn baby brother Titan. **FML**

Today, I was helping an old man find a pair of shoes. I told him about a particularly comfortable pair, but had to inform him that they only came in black or white. Hearing this, the old man grabbed me by the neck and began to beat me around the head with our display shoe. He wanted brown. **FML**

✱

Today, I went to a club and my friends and I got up on the stage, but security told me to get down, saying the stage was only for girls. I'm twenty-three. I'm a girl. **FML**

✱

Today, I was carrying my mug of hot chocolate. When I arrived in the living room, my sleeve got caught on the door handle. **FML**

Today, I crashed my car into a ditch on my way home from work. I had to walk two miles in the freezing cold before I could get a mobile signal to call the AA. When I got back to my car, a cop was waiting for me with a ticket for leaving the scene of an accident. **FML**

*

Today, I was watching a porn video on my laptop when my mum walked into my room, so I slammed the laptop shut. The speakers continue to function after the laptop is closed. **FML**

*

Today, it's my birthday, but I had to go to work. I caught the train and was forced to sit next to this weird, smelly guy, who got off one stop before mine. A little old lady jumped on so I shuffled over so she could sit down with ease. Upon exiting the train, I noticed my trousers were wet with the guy's piss. **FML**

Today, a girl was coming on to me and buying me drinks during a concert. At the end of the evening, she gave me her number so that we could go out. Because of the booze, I forgot it. **FML**

Today, I danced with a girl until the bar closed. We went back to my place. She had a penis. **FML**

Today, my father asked me if he could borrow my electric razor because he wanted to 'surprise Mum later'. Anxious to see him without his lifelong beard, I willingly agreed. Half an hour later, he exited the bathroom – beard fully intact. **FML**

*

Today, a man on the train asked me if I had any change. I quickly responded with, '*No habla ingles*' ('I don't speak English'). He then tapped me on the shoulder and said, 'That would've been a lot more believable if you weren't reading that paper.' **FML**

Today, it took me over three hours to cut out little letters for an event I'm putting on. It took the wind less than a second to blow them all over campus. **FML**

Today, I went to the movies with a friend and her grandma. Her grandma was using toothpicks and carelessly dropping them on the ground. I took a big handful of popcorn from the bucket on the floor, and got a piece of her toothpick lodged in my throat. **FML**

*

Today, I stood by the wall at a party while everyone else danced and ignored me. It was my birthday party. **FML**

Today, while out to lunch, my sister called me and asked me to pick her up from town. I told her she'd have to wait. She got pissed off and started cursing me, so I hung up on her. She called me back thirty-seven times until I answered and yelled, 'WILL YOU LEAVE ME THE FUCK ALONE?' It was my boss. **FML**

✳

Today, after some very passionate sex with my girlfriend, she exclaimed, 'That was amazing, Drew ...' She quickly tried to turn 'Drew' into my actual name, which does not sound a thing like Drew. **FML**

✳

Today, I fell flat on my back while running for the train, only to find out that it was standing there for ten minutes. I rode to work with a train full of people who had watched me fall. **FML**

✳

Today, I was on a date with a pretty girl. I attempted to put my arm around her, but elbowed her in the face instead. **FML**

✳

Today, I fell from the top of the stairs, caught myself in the middle, stood up, stepped down one more, tripped and fell down the rest. **FML**

✳

Today, I left work and, because of the nice weather, decided to walk home across town. Only when I entered my flat did I notice that the bottom of my mini-skirt was tucked into my knickers. **FML**

Today, I found out just how thin the walls of my new student flat are. They are so thin, in fact, that I can hear the creepy guy next door say my full name over and over again very slowly while masturbating vigorously. **FML**

*

Today, I was standing on a desk at work changing a light bulb, since we had no ladder. My phone rang, I rushed to answer it, tripped and smashed my leg. It was my boss, calling to tell me he was bringing a ladder. **FML**

*

Today, I was staying with my grandmother and overheard her having phone sex. **FML**

*

Today, I was looking after my parents' house and their dog, and fell asleep on the couch. The dog proceeded to climb on my shoulders and rest behind my head like a doggie pillow. She farted right in my left ear. **FML**

*

Today, I was going on a tropical holiday with my boyfriend and his family. When we got to the airport, security stopped me and opened my carry-on bag. I'd forgotten about the no-liquids rule. They took out a bottle of lube, Vagisil and Veet. His whole family saw. **FML**

*

Today, I farted at my desk, thinking no one would smell it. Two seconds later, everyone came over to wish me a happy birthday. **FML**

Today, I came home early from work and discovered my husband wearing a black baby-doll nightdress, black stockings and high heels. He says it helps him to relax. **FML**

Today, at seven in the morning, I ended up outside in a nightgown, barefoot and in the pouring rain. I've just found out that my two-year-old son now knows how to close the patio door, which, of course, has no exterior handle. **FML**

Today, I was having sex with my boyfriend. When he was about to orgasm, he screamed, 'Yes, Brittany!' at the top of his lungs. My name's not Brittany. That's his sister. **FML**

Today, I was volunteering at a nursing home and I was calling bingo numbers. When one woman stood up and started making noises, I assumed she had won and I started clapping. She fell on the floor and died of a heart attack. I essentially applauded her death. **FML**

Today, I was having sex with a guy that I'd just met. I thought he was having an orgasm; he was actually having an asthma attack. **FML**

✱

Today, I was walking in the snow and saw a kid slip. I laughed and felt good about myself. Then I fell. **FML**

✱

Today, my airline lost my luggage when I flew back from France. They lost my luggage when I flew to France. **FML**

✱

Today, for the first time, I got it on with this man I like. He took his shirt off to reveal a chest full of black hair. His name was shaved into it. **FML**

Today, a really hot guy walked into my office. Wanting to impress him, I picked up the phone and pretended to be making a huge business deal, talking loudly about big sums of money. I put the phone down and smiled seductively at him. He said, 'Hi! I'm here to connect your phone lines.' **FML**

Today, I fell asleep. I felt something on my face. I batted it away. It was my hamster. It died from hitting the wall. **FML**

Today, I was eating ice cream and I noticed some on my jeans, so I wiped it off with my finger and licked it. It was bird shit. **FML**

✳

Today, I decided to send my boyfriend a picture text of me naked. I accidentally sent it to my dad. He sent a text back saying, 'You definitely take after your mum.' **FML**

✳

Today, I was awarding medals to finalists in a school club. While putting one around one girl's neck, I ended up poking her in the eye. She tried to walk back across the stage, but her eyes were watering too much. She missed the step and fell, breaking her ankle. **FML**

Today, I took a picture for my photography course of a random couple kissing in the snow from afar. Later, upon closer inspection, I realized that the guy was my boyfriend. **FML**

*

Today, I woke up to find my car covered in shaving cream and tampons and the word 'cheater' written across my windscreen in lipstick. The guy a few doors down from me has the same car as me. I'm a virgin. **FML**

*

Today, while my four-year-old nephew was hugging me, he stepped back and declared, 'Auntie, my willy is hard. Will it go away?' **FML**

*

Today, I went to my first strip club for my friend's birthday. I also found out what my girlfriend does for a living. **FML**

*

Today, my boyfriend was really stressed about a guy he works with being an idiot. I told him, 'If you ignore something long enough, it won't bother you anymore.' His response was: 'I've ignored my herpes for a long time, but it still bothers me.' We've been having sex for three months. **FML**

*

Today, I woke up at five and studied for my 9.30 a.m. exam for four hours. When I left my house at nine, it was dark outside. Turns out I slept through the entire day and woke up at 5 p.m. **FML**

Today, I went to my car to discover an apologetic note on the windscreen from the council, telling me that they had hit my car. On top of that note was a parking ticket, also from the council. **FML**

*

Today, my friend was picking on me at school by constantly tapping me on the shoulder. By break, I'd had enough. I felt the familiar tap on my shoulder and drove my elbow into his stomach. It was the head teacher. **FML**

*

Today, I bit into my egg sandwich. When I looked down at it, there were five long, grey hairs leading from the sandwich into my mouth. **FML**

*

Today, while photocopying some stuff for school, I felt someone rubbing her boobs against my back. I got a boner. When I looked to see who she was, I saw my fat friend rubbing his man boobs against my back. **FML**

*

Today, I found out that I am being sued for losing a set of wedding photos that I took. I lost them when I was mugged on the way home from the shoot, when £10,000 worth of equipment was also stolen from me. **FML**

*

Today, I wanted to seduce my boyfriend, so I put on my sexiest lingerie and played some romantic music. As he was eating dinner, I climbed up on the table and started seductively crawling across to him. The table collapsed. **FML**

Today, my tattoo artist boyfriend of five months gave me my first tattoo in celebration of my eighteenth birthday. It was supposed to be a heart with my name in script. He spelled my name wrong. **FML**

✱

Today, while I was working at a cafe, a tall, well-dressed man came in and ordered. After I'd served him, I asked him why he was dressed so nicely. He responded, 'I'm going to court for stalking pretty girls like you.' **FML**

✱

Today, I had to tell my super-conservative parents that I had just gone to visit the boyfriend I'm not supposed to have, so that I could tell him I am pregnant. **FML**

Today, my grandma was showing me an ancient family letter. It was apparently written by someone historically famous. She was going on about how important it was, in such good condition too, worth a lot. I dropped my glass of juice. It spilled all over it. **FML**

Today, I dropped my iPhone on the supermarket floor and shattered the screen. I managed, however, to catch the macaroni cheese before it hit the ground. **FML**

Today, I walked into my room to find that my mum had made my bed and done my laundry, for which I thanked her with a hug. I then lay down on the bed, stretched out my arms ... and realized my vibrator was still under the pillow where I had left it. **FML**

*

Today, my first real date ended with the girl saying, 'Thanks for dinner, I was hungry – and oh, by the way, I'm a lesbian.' **FML**

Today, I was looking after a hamster for a friend. My dog ate it. **FML**

119

Today, I was at work at the Disney Store. A small boy was curled in a ball on the floor, crying, so I went over to him. After talking to him for a little while, I discovered he couldn't find his mother. Once he'd calmed down, I helped him stand up. He choked back his tears and then puked all over me from the waist down. **FML**

*

Today, I went to give a blood sample for the first time. After I explained to the nurse how nervous I was, she replied, 'Oh, don't worry! This is my first time too!' **FML**

*

Today, the hard drive on my computer crashed with all of my files on it. I took it to my dad, who is a computer analyst, to see if he could recover anything. The only thing that he could salvage was my extensive collection of porn. **FML**

*

Today, I was giving a PowerPoint presentation at school. I had forgotten that my boyfriend had changed my desktop picture the night before. I plugged in the wire that connects my computer to the projector, opened my laptop … and projected a huge picture of me nude onto the wall. I go to a Catholic school. **FML**

*

Today, my boyfriend's sister called to wish me congratulations and ask me when I was due. I said I wasn't pregnant, to which she replied, 'Yes you are, my brother just told us the good news.' Long pause. 'Oh wait, is this Mary or Morgan?' I'm Morgan. Who's Mary? **FML**

Today, I left my glasses at home. While walking to the bus stop, I saw the most beautiful girl on the street smiling and waving at me from her front garden. I happily waved back, smiling, and kept going. It turned out that she was crying and calling me over. Her dad had just had a heart attack. **FML**

*

Today, while I was working, my ex-girlfriend came in to apply for a job. She broke up with me for another guy so I can't stand being in the same room as her. The manager hired her on the spot. I have to train her. **FML**

Today, a customer that I've been waiting on for years came into the restaurant after a long absence. I said to him, 'Hey, it looks like you've lost a lot of weight! How'd you do it?' He replied, 'I've got cancer.' **FML**

Today, I had to wear a mouse costume for a children's party. Due to the disgusting smell and heat in the costume, I fainted. I awoke to a little boy screaming, who then proceeded to kick me in the face and run. **FML**

*

Today, my boyfriend and I discreetly ordered sex toys online and requested that they be delivered to my flat. They were sent to the billing address in error. It's my parents' credit card. **FML**

Today, I was eating crisps with my niece when I started to feel that some were wet. I looked at my niece and noticed that she was sucking on them and then putting them back in the bag. **FML**

*

Today, I borrowed a van to move some of my furniture. I wasn't used to the brakes, so when I stopped at a red light, I pretty much ended up on the pedestrian crossing. Suddenly, I heard a loud thud at the side of the van. I turned to see what idiot would walk into a van. It was a blind man. **FML**

Today, while driving, I hit a car as I was trying to answer a phone call. Frustrated, I answered the phone and shouted, 'What?!' To which my mother replied, 'I just had a bad feeling in my gut about you, so I wanted to make sure you were OK.' **FML**

Today, my family gathered for my ninety-six-year-old great-grandmother's surprise birthday party, which was my idea. When she walked in, we surprised her so much that she had a heart attack. She is now in hospital. **FML**

*

Today, two days before my birthday, my parents drove three hours to visit me at university and take me out to lunch. I assumed that it was to celebrate my birthday. They told me they are getting divorced. **FML**

Today, I woke up and felt like I had to throw up. The closest bathroom to mine is the one in my parents' room, so I ran in there – without knocking. I walked in on my parents having sex. Shocked, I gasped for air and threw up all over their bed. **FML**

*

Today, I was at the beach with my friend. Messing around, he swam up behind me and dunked me under the water. Naturally, moments later, I swam up behind him, grabbed both his ankles and stood up, flipping him completely – only to see him watching me from a few feet away. I flipped a seventy-year-old man. **FML**

Today, my mum bought me a T-shirt. It has the US Marines' logo on it and says: 'Marine's Girlfriend'. I'm a straight sixteen-year-old boy. My mum reads and speaks only Spanish. **FML**

Today, I discovered that my flatmate has been using my loofah to clean our toilet. I've been cleaning myself with the shit of four men for the last six months. **FML**

*

Today, I laced up my fabulous new boots and went outside to find my cute neighbour. Feeling quite confident, I struck a pose for him. But then, walking down the front steps, I fell arse over tit. I woke up hours later – with seven stitches in my head. **FML**

*

Today, I was in the changing room at the local swimming pool. I went to use the public hairdryer, but couldn't – because a naked old man was already there, bent over, butt cheeks spread wide with his hands, and bum aimed squarely at the dryer. He was enjoying it. **FML**

*

Today, at the dentist, I was getting my teeth cleaned. Looking up at the dentist's nose, I saw runny snot dripping onto his lip. I tried to move away slowly. He told me, 'Stop!' The movement of his lips caused the snot to fall right into my mouth. **FML**

*

Today, I went to A & E with severe pain in my abdominal area. The doctor came in after looking at the CAT scan and said, 'Well, it's not your appendix.' Thinking I was in the clear, I said, 'That's awesome.' The doctor then responded with, 'It's probably your testicles.' **FML**

Today, I overheard my parents having sex. Trying to be the reasonable person I am, I dismissed it, appreciating that sex is normal. I walked quickly past their room, but just at that moment my cat ran straight past me and into their room, cracking open the door on his way inside. My parents now think I was peeping and need counselling. **FML**

✳

Today, I was working in a shop when an elderly woman asked me if I could help her find her favourite bra. I proceeded to ask what brand it was and she replied, 'I'll check the tag.' She lifted up the front of her shirt and flipped one cup of her bra inside out. I saw everything. **FML**

✳

Today, I was going for a job interview on my birthday. I had a shirt and a tie on and I had my BlackBerry in my pocket. I was running a little late so I dashed outside. When I came out of the door, a bunch of my mates screamed 'Happy Birthday!' and poured Coke all over me. **FML**

✳

Today, I was going to a *Harry Potter* convention as I love the books so much. On my drive there, I got lost. Things only got worse when my car broke down. Since I'd forgotten my phone, I decided to try to hitch a lift. I stood by the side of the road for two hours, dressed as Ron Weasley. **FML**

✳

Today, I scored the winning goal in the cup final. For the other team. **FML**

Today, I was meeting my sister's fiancé for the first time. I stopped at an Internet cafe on the way to her house for dinner. I was on a computer and there was a really attractive man next to me. We flirted and exchanged numbers. Turns out, he was my sister's fiancé. **FML**

*

Today, I came home early from work to surprise my son with a new mountain bike for his birthday. To keep it a surprise, I carried it quietly up to his bedroom. As I opened the door, I heard my son say, 'Oh man, you're gonna make me come,' to the girl he was on top of. He just turned fourteen. **FML**

Today, I decided to do a load of laundry. A minute into the cycle, as the water started to drip into the machine, I realized that I'd left my iPod in my jeans pocket. The washing-machine door locks automatically and cannot be opened until the forty-minute cycle is up. **FML**

Today, I decided to lighten my hair. I applied the dye and waited twenty minutes. When I went to wash the dye out, the water wouldn't turn on. After my head started to burn, I called the landlord in a panic. A pipe had burst and the entire neighbourhood didn't have water. **FML**

Today, I had a job interview. I stopped for a pee in the lobby before I went in. I relaxed a bit too much at the urinal and accidentally farted. I proceeded to chuckle about it like a five-year-old for a few seconds. The guy next to me at the urinal turned out to be the interviewer. **FML**

✱

Today, I woke up to find that the large container of leftover beef stroganoff that I put down the waste disposal last night had backed up into my bath. **FML**

Today, my mum brought my dog in to wake me up. He jumped up on the bed. I started to pet what I thought was his neck and play with a random tuft of fur. I soon realized that it was his penis. **FML**

Today, I was taking the train to college. It was about 6.30 a.m. and I was listening to music and catching up on some homework. I took my headphones off for a second to adjust them. While they were off, I heard some grunting and looked over at the man across from me. He was masturbating. **FML**

✱

Today, I was arrested because my six-year-old son called the police to say that I was hitting my wife and she was crying. My wife and I were having sex. **FML**

Today, I went outside for a late-night cigarette. When I opened the door and took one step back inside, all I remember is a big thud. I woke up five minutes later to find my father standing over me, saying, 'Nice right hook, eh?' Then he chuckled. He'd thought I was a burglar. He'd knocked me out. **FML**

*

Today, I was sitting in my maths class when I glanced over to the other side of the room, where the hottest girl in school was sitting. I could see her thong so I instantly got a boner. About a minute later, my teacher called me up to the board to solve a problem. **FML**

*

Today, I tried to prove to my dad that he snores by secretly putting a tape recorder under his bed. I soon found out my parents had sex that night. My mum likes to talk dirty. **FML**

Today, my mum came to me and asked if I had drunk her wine. I'm sixteen, so I lied and said no. The next morning, there was a tape on my bed labelled: 'Security cameras – love Mum.' It was a video of me downing her red wine and having sex with my boyfriend. **FML**

Today, I'm twenty and I'm going bald. **FML**

Today, I took my dog for a walk down by the river. I was throwing sticks for him with one hand and talking on the phone with the other. Then I threw my phone in the river and stood there talking to the stick. **FML**

Today, I was watching a movie with my boyfriend and his parents. It got to an intense sex scene. I felt grateful when I saw his father reaching for the remote to fast-forward the scene. He put it into slow motion by accident. We watched in silence for about three minutes until he managed to fix it. **FML**

*

Today, I was woken up by the sound of power tools at 6.30 a.m. I stuck my head out of my window and yelled at them to shut up. They didn't stop. So I walked out my front door to find the bastards. It was firemen. They were sawing down the door of my neighbour's burning house. **FML**

Today, I was on the train. I have fairly serious
OCD so I avoid holding the poles or handles. All
the seats were taken, so I leaned against a wall.
At the next stop, this obese, sweaty man got on
and grabbed the two poles around me, effectively
hugging me. My shirt was wet when he left. **FML**

∗

Today, as I was walking my friend's dog, I noticed
a little girl fall off her bike. I let go of the dog
and ran over to help. The girl was fine – but the
dog ran into the road and was hit by a truck. **FML**

∗

Today, I checked my Facebook to find I had been
tagged in a bunch of photos from a party I
attended last night. On each picture, I had a
comment from my mum saying, 'You're
grounded.' **FML**

∗

Today, I texted my boyfriend to tell him how
terrible I felt about cheating. He replied to say he
was so relieved to get my message because he
had been cheating on me with another girl. I was
talking about my maths exam. **FML**

∗

Today, the phone rang while I was home alone.
When I picked it up, all I could hear was heavy
breathing. Convinced it was one of my friends
playing a joke, I said loudly, 'Get off the phone,
you fucker, and don't call back!' It turned out it
was my grandma – having a stroke. **FML**

∗∗∗

LOWER THAN LOW

Today, I realized that the dog humping my leg was the most action I've had in months. **FML**

Today, I was talking to my friend about my life and she stopped me mid-sentence and told me that my life makes her sad. **FML**

＊

Today, I confronted my fiancé and told him I knew his 'little secret'. I had suspected that he had been ruining his wedding diet by eating pizza at the office. He replied that the affair with his secretary had only been going on for a couple of months. **FML**

＊

Today, I signed up for an online dating site. After completing their personality quiz, I set the distance to a sixty-mile radius of where I live. Then to the country. Then to the whole world. I got no matches for any of the settings. **FML**

Today, I got an email from the local Dungeons & Dragons group to say that the next meeting will be on 14 February. I don't know what is more sad: that the group is meeting on Valentine's Day, or that I have nothing better to do but go. **FML**

Today, it's my birthday. It's 6.30 p.m. and I'm still the only person aware of what day it is. **FML**

*

Today, I organized a romantic evening with one of my old squeezes in the hope of reigniting something special. She showed up at eight and told me she had to leave by nine. She was gone by eight-thirty. **FML**

*

Today, I'm twenty years old and have never been kissed. **FML**

*

Today, I got an email from a guy I'd once had a one-night stand with. He wanted to get together to talk about it. Turns out, he's in rehab and wants to address the biggest mistakes he's ever made in his life. I am on a drug addict's list of regrets. **FML**

*

Today, I cut myself with childproof scissors. **FML**

Today, I'm so lethargic at work that the light in my office, which comes on via a motion detector, went off. **FML**

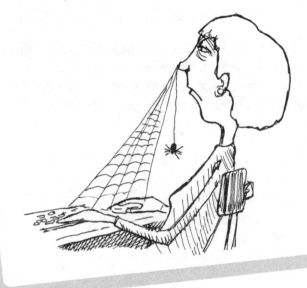

Today, I sat next to a truly bootylicious babe. I was feeling nervous, but I managed to ask her shyly for her phone number. It was only when I arrived back home that I realized there was a digit missing. **FML**

*

Today, I met the girl who dumped me because the distance between us was too great. We're in the same city again. She's now dating a Marine based in Iraq. **FML**

Today, I yelled while I was sleeping. I was sleeping during a very important meeting with all the customers and my boss. **FML**

*

Today, I kissed the girl I love for the first time. Her reaction? She threw up. **FML**

*

Today, my boyfriend was tapping on my thigh to the beat of the music as we were driving to dinner. When I asked him what he was doing, he replied, 'Just watching the ripples.' **FML**

*

Today, I'm a French girl in England, and a cute boy asks me where I'm from exactly. When I tell him Paris, he answers, 'Strange – I always heard Parisians were the most beautiful women in the world.' **FML**

*

Today, I went to have a drink with my friend. On the way, I withdrew £40. When I arrived at the bar, I realized I had taken my card from the machine – but not the money. **FML**

*

Today, I woke up after being rushed in for emergency surgery because of an infected gall bladder. When I woke up, the first thing I saw was a disgusting-looking lumpy thing in a pot by my bed. It was the offending gallstone. My surgeon thought I might like to keep it, as a 'memento'. **FML**

Today, my boss sneezed onto his hands, and then licked them in front of my best customers. **FML**

*

Today, I pointed out to my girlfriend that she wasn't the jealous type. She replied, 'Well, actually, I am – I just can't prove it because no one else is interested in you.' **FML**

*

Today, I helped my son do his maths homework. He got a C and won't talk to me anymore. **FML**

*

Today, it's my birthday. Before my girlfriend gave me the present she had bought for me, I jokingly said, 'I hope it's not a tie!' It was. **FML**

Today, my fourteen-year-old little sister asked me how I'd felt when I'd had my first sexual experience. I told her it was personal and none of her business. She then looked at me and said, 'I thought it was nice.' I'm nineteen and a virgin. **FML**

Today, my girlfriend came home with new condoms – 'Extended Pleasure' – containing a numbing gel designed to help me last longer. **FML**

Today, my boyfriend of almost a year told me he thinks he might be gay. I took off my shirt, climbed over him sexily and began to kiss him passionately. 'What do you think now?' I asked seductively. His response? 'Now I'm sure I'm gay.' **FML**

*

Today, as I was doing it with my girlfriend, she asked, 'Are you finished any time soon?' **FML**

*

Today, I asked my girlfriend if she wanted to go to the cinema. She replied, 'Sorry, I have to do stuff with my parents.' Her mum then called and by mistake my girlfriend hit speakerphone. The first thing her mum said was: 'Be back at eleven.' **FML**

*

Today, it's 2.23 in the morning, and my drunken girlfriend has just called me from a party where she's the only girl there. She seems to be having a great time. **FML**

*

Today, my girlfriend made fun of me, saying that I'm too emotional, which really pissed me off, so I started shouting at her to show her that I'm 'all man' ... which made me start crying. **FML**

*

Today, I aimed at the little blue disc placed at the bottom of the urinal. I learned the hard way that when it splashes off, it makes little blue stains on trousers. **FML**

Today, someone I used to know got in touch with me. I hadn't heard from him in years. He insisted that we meet up as soon as possible, and asked me to go to his house that afternoon. I spent the afternoon repairing his computer, and haven't heard from him since. **FML**

Today, I discovered that there is a security camera in the storage room at my work. The same room where, two days ago, I masturbated. **FML**

Today, I went to a speed-dating event. After seven minutes, the girl told me she wasn't interested. I asked her at what point of the conversation she had made up her mind, and she answered, 'When you said, "Hello." Goodbye.' **FML**

Today, I turned around to see the entire marketing department getting ready to have lunch together. Nobody mentioned it to me. **FML**

*

Today, I was in the cafeteria when I noticed a new worker cleaning a table. As I passed her, she looked up and smiled at me. Thinking she was pulling a funny face, I jokingly crossed my eyes and smiled back. She looked hurt and continued working. Later, she served me my lunch. She was actually cross-eyed. **FML**

Today, I got a letter of acceptance from Oxford University. I jumped for joy, screaming at the top of my lungs. My little brother then walked in with his camcorder, laughing, and handed me the real letter. I was turned down. **FML**

Today, I went out for lunch with two old school friends. We saw a girl who had also been at school with us. The girl gave both of them hugs and introduced herself to me. **FML**

*

Today, I just realized that the colleague I refused to leave my wife for is happily married to someone else. I'm now divorced. **FML**

*

Today, I found dark hairs growing on my chest, nipples and stomach. I'm a nineteen-year-old girl. **FML**

Today, though I'm normally unperturbed by my single status, I walked by some squirrels engaged in mating rituals and felt a pang of jealousy. **FML**

✱

Today, I told my boyfriend that I didn't like his facial hair and that he should shave it off. He replied, 'You first.' **FML**

✱

Today, I passed by a clothes shop and decided to go in to look at the jeans. Before I could even step through the door, the shop owner told me expressionlessly, 'All the sizes here are too small for you.' **FML**

✱

Today, my boyfriend told me I smell like vegetables. **FML**

✱

Today, I regret that break my ex and I took. I thought it would lead him to realize that he wanted to stop flirting and cheating with other girls and be with only me for ever. Now I'm the girl he cheats on his girlfriend with. **FML**

✱

Today, my mum asked all the old ladies in her church to pray that I meet 'someone special'. **FML**

✱

Today, I was trying to finish an English assignment but was foxed about how to complete it. So I emailed my teacher asking for advice, and she responded, 'Flip over the handout for instructions.' **FML**

Today, I daringly tried that fish bath thing – where the fish come to you and eat all of your skin's dead cells. I submerged myself in it and after fifteen minutes of me being a human buffet, twenty of the fish had died. **FML**

✱

Today, I told the man I love to 'go first' when we started talking at the same time. I wanted to confess my feelings; he wanted to tell me about his engagement. **FML**

✱

Today, I've been dating a girl for a year and she's only touched my penis twice. Once was by accident. **FML**

Today, my brother's girlfriend dumped him. I overheard my mum telling him, 'It could be worse – your brother can't even get a girlfriend.' **FML**

Today, I realized that I know more about the Transformers' history than I do about talking to women. **FML**

✱

Today, I went to buy some soap. This seventy-year-old woman next to me asked a sales assistant if they had any bubble bath mix. I found myself picturing her naked, bathing herself, and suddenly my dick just couldn't sit still. I haven't had sex in over twenty-two months. **FML**

Today, I sent a Facebook friend request to my ex. This afternoon, I noticed that she had accepted, and had left a message for me in my inbox – asking how she knew me. **FML**

*

Today, I had to walk home from school in the rain because my mum 'didn't have a car to pick me up in'. When I got home, there was a car in the driveway. **FML**

*

Today, I am contemplating ending my relationship of six years. My boyfriend is too busy playing *Guitar Hero* to listen. **FML**

*

Today, my boss was walking towards me, screaming about how she was 'so tired' of my 'bullshit'. So I proceeded to tell her how much I hate her and how she should go lose some pounds. Turns out, she was talking to her husband via her Bluetooth headset. **FML**

*

Today, I sneezed so hard I herniated my back. After passing out from the pain, I awoke on the floor, covered in my own shit and piss. Unable to move, I had to wait in this state for four hours until my wife returned home from work, cleaned me up and took me to hospital. **FML**

*

Today, I hid my credit card from myself so I wouldn't use it. Now I can't find it. **FML**

Today, I was talking to my parents about feeling insecure about my 'beach body' as summer gets closer and closer. My dad's advice was: 'Don't wear a grey swimsuit. People will try to roll you back into the ocean.' **FML**

Today, I was on the phone to my boyfriend for over an hour, listening to him talk about his new car and his final exams. I literally did not say one word. Just as I said, 'Hey baby, guess what happened to me today?' he said, 'Can I go to sleep? I'm too tired to guess. 'Night,' and hung up. **FML**

*

Today, I gathered the courage to participate in a class discussion. My teacher laughed at me. **FML**

144

Today, I woke up at 5.15 a.m., shovelled and salted the driveway for over an hour, left early and drove an hour on shitty roads to get to work on time, only to be laid off. **FML**

＊

Today, on my eighteenth birthday, my mum told me the man I thought was my father for my whole life was actually not my father. My real father is in prison for murder. **FML**

＊

Today, I went into work and told my boss that I hated my job and was quitting. I tried to rush out, but I slipped and fell on the marble floor in front of the whole office. **FML**

Today, the girl on whom I have had a crush for two years snuck up behind me to give me a hug. I farted very loudly at the exact same moment. **FML**

Today, I realized I bought thirty condoms one year ago. I now have twenty-nine. **FML**

＊

Today, I was with the guy I am seeing and we were fooling around in my room. I proposed sex. He said he didn't have time because he had to play *Mario Kart*. **FML**

Today, the guy I fancy was having a party. After a few sips of my Green Apple Smirnoff, I puked up the Chinese food I had eaten earlier – all over his new couch, in front of him and a bunch of strangers. **FML**

*

Today, I masturbated three times to the thought of my wife because we don't have sex anymore. **FML**

*

Today, I had a wet dream. When I woke up, I was touching myself. I also woke up to find that I had fallen asleep on the couch after eating too much turkey at a family reunion. Over twenty relatives were giving me nasty looks. **FML**

*

Today, I asked a guy out for a coffee and we started talking about our mutual careers. At the end of the date, he asked me if I had any more questions about job opportunities or any more advice, then shook my hand and gave me his card. **FML**

*

Today, my fiancé told me that he no longer loves me, and that he still has feelings for an ex. The wedding is off and he needs the ring back to give to the right woman. **FML**

*

Today, my four-year-old niece asked me why I didn't have a job or a wife. **FML**

Today, I was singing to my cat and she reached up and put her paw over my mouth. **FML**

✱

Today, I listened to my flatmate having sex from 3 a.m. until 6 a.m. When I looked over at my girlfriend, who must have thought I was asleep, I noticed she was masturbating. **FML**

Today was the first time I ever saw a vagina 'in person'. It was during med school training on how to do a pelvic exam. **FML**

Today, I found a used condom and wrapper in the bathroom bin at my girlfriend's house. The condom is not a brand I've ever used. She lives alone. **FML**

✱

Today, at the school where I teach, the kids all voted for their favourite teacher. I was the only one to receive zero votes. When I asked a small group of students why no one voted for me, one boy replied, 'Because you're the ugliest.' **FML**

✱

Today, my girlfriend dumped me, proclaiming she wanted someone more like 'her Edward'. I asked her who Edward was. She held up a copy of her *Twilight* book. She was talking about a fictional vampire. **FML**

Today, my phone rang for the first time in four days. It was my mum. She'd dialled the wrong number. **FML**

*

Today, I discovered a secret drawer in my house full of chocolates, biscuits, cakes and pastries. When I asked my sister about it, she told me that the entire family knew about the drawer, but that my mum had thought it would be a good idea to hide the fattening foods from me. **FML**

*

Today, I woke up at around 5 a.m. after a party I threw last night. I was still quite drunk. This girl was lying next to me from the night before. I kissed her, and about a minute and a half into it, she opened her eyes and said, 'Oh, it's you,' then got up and walked out. **FML**

*

Today, I drove my girlfriend home at around 11 p.m. We put the car in her garage, where we started to have sex. When she climaxed, she slipped and hit her head. Her parents heard the crash and came down. We were both naked. She was unconscious. **FML**

*

Today, having just told me what a great job I've been doing and how he'd really like to start giving me some more responsibility, my boss asked me if I'd sharpen a couple of pencils for him. **FML**

*

Today, I am finally dating the girl I have liked on and off for the past year. In the school play. **FML**

Today, a creepy man on the Tube said he liked my eyeballs. It was the best compliment I'd received in months. **FML**

Today, a flight attendant asked me if I was airsick because I looked really pale. I told her that was my normal complexion, but thanked her for her concern. She insisted, 'No, that can't be normal.' **FML**

*

Today, I can't decide what's worse: my mum walking in on me pleasuring myself, or the one-hour talk the following day about how it's perfectly normal and even she does it. **FML**

Today, my sister teased me about being a mistake. When I told my mum what my sister had said, her response was: 'I still love you anyway.' **FML**

*

Today, I made a joke about my wedding to my mum and she told me not to joke about something that will probably never happen. **FML**

*

Today, I met up with some old friends from school. It was great to see everyone all grown-up and to hear their stories. Before leaving, we decided to have a group photo for old times' sake. They asked me to take the picture. **FML**

*

Today, I put my picture into a celebrity lookalike website. The three matches that came up were Barbra Streisand, Hillary Clinton and Boy George. I'm sixteen. I'm a boy. **FML**

*

Today, I received my passport in the post. They'd got my birth date wrong. Then I picked up my birth certificate, which I had sent in with the application. Turns out, my parents have been celebrating my birthday on the wrong day for sixteen years. **FML**

*

Today, in my science class, I was sitting next to my friend Jill. My teacher always gets our names confused, calling me Jill and her Liz. She decided to combine our names. I'm now known as Jizz. My teacher clearly has no idea what it means. **FML**

Today, I was giving my boyfriend a blow job. He was twitching and moving around and saying, 'Oh yeah.' Then he said, 'Take that, bitch.' I looked up – to see he was only excited about how he was dominating in *Call of Duty 4*. **FML**

✱

Today, I submitted my picture to a dating website. It was rejected because I didn't clarify which person I was. The picture was of me and my dog. **FML**

✱

Today, I took a friend out for what I thought was a date. After dinner was over and I'd paid, she pulled the bill out and wrote her name and phone number on it for the waiter. **FML**

✱

Today, my girlfriend and I were watching a show about sex on the Discovery Channel. The topic of female orgasms came up and she said, 'Wow, I wonder what that's like?' We've been sexually active for three years. **FML**

✱

Today, I was complaining to my mum about how my sister looks like a Barbie doll next to me. I was saying how she is so tanned and her hair looks great next to mine. Mum paused for a while and then said, 'Well, you're pretty on the inside.' **FML**

✱

Today, I was having sex with a girl I really like for the first time. After a while, I told her I was about to come. Her response: 'Lucky you.' **FML**

Today, I was happy because my exact shirt and jumper were in a fashion magazine. Until I looked closer: they were in the 'what not to wear' category. **FML**

*

Today, I told my college friend that I considered her to be my best friend. She responded, 'I don't think you should call me that.' **FML**

*

Today, my boyfriend of two years sent me a text message saying, 'Don't worry, I'm gonna break up with her soon. Love you.' **FML**

*

Today, my head teacher called me into his office to talk. He asked me if I was new because it seemed like I was having trouble making friends. I've been at the school for four years. **FML**

*

Today, I took a test in controlled conditions as part of a job interview. I took a sip from a bottle of juice, and the lady leading the test gave me a warning. I tried to explain that if I didn't, I would faint. She took the bottle and hid it. Fifteen minutes later, I collapsed. She thought I was faking. I'm hypoglycaemic. **FML**

*

Today, at the end of a really long day, my boyfriend was rubbing my back. I told him I appreciated how sensitive he was being. His response? 'I was just trying to figure out how to unhook your bra.' **FML**

Today, I kneeled down to tie my shoe and sneezed, nailing my face on my knee and breaking my nose. **FML**

*

Today, I got fired from a great babysitting job because the little girl said I was boring. **FML**

*

Today, I was watching a documentary on the world's fattest man. Halfway through the show, the reporter started talking about the man's girlfriend. The fattest man in the world has a girlfriend. I'm twenty-one and have never had a girlfriend. **FML**

Today, I was walking home from work when a woman asked me to come inside for a free meal. It was a homeless shelter. **FML**

Today, I got my fake ID and went out. One of my friends asked to see my ID. He noticed that my birthday didn't make me over eighteen. I paid £50 for a fake ID with my real birthday on. **FML**

*

Today, I asked to borrow my fat friend's trousers for an interview tomorrow. I figured I'd just get a belt to hold them up. They fit. **FML**

Today, I realized that there are more framed pictures of my mum's dog than there are pictures of me around the house. **FML**

Today, my boyfriend broke up with me. I cried and told him that I loved him. He gave me 20p and told me to call someone who cared. I threw the money in his face and ran. I waited for the bus, but when I got on, I realized I was 20p short of the fare. I walked home in the rain. **FML**

Today, I decided to introduce my girlfriend to my parents and told them that we were going to have a very special guest for dinner. While my mum was preparing the meal, she asked, 'What food does he like?' I'm straight. My parents thought differently. **FML**

✳

Today, my boyfriend gave me a card for my birthday and told me to open it ten minutes after he'd left. I waited five. Inside the card, the message read: 'It's not working out, but here's £20.' **FML**

✳

Today, the girl I like mentioned that she was home alone and was really, really lonely. She asked me to come over and watch a few movies with her. Just as I was about to leave for her place, she sent me a text saying, 'Can you pick up my friend Spencer on the way?' **FML**

Today, I found out my ex-girlfriend put Nair in my shampoo before moving out. I'm now bald. **FML**

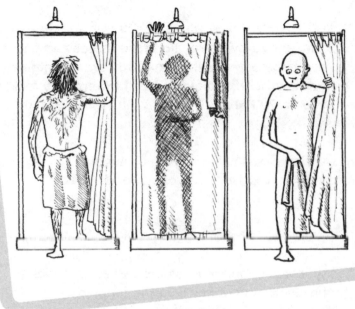

Today, I went to the doctors and the nurse asked if I was married, to which I responded, 'Yes.' She then asked if I was sexually active. 'No.' **FML**

✱

Today, my mum walked in on me looking at a 1978 *Playboy*. She asked if I found it in the basement. I said yes. Then I realized she was the centrefold. **FML**

✱

Today, I told a girl I liked her. She replied, 'Don't.' **FML**

Today, my boyfriend asked me what I had enjoyed most about the weekend we'd just spent together. I mentioned in detail a certain move he had pulled during sex. When I asked him what he'd enjoyed the most, he replied, 'Putting my fish tank together.' **FML**

*

Today, I was walking along the street and passed a young couple. Behind me, I heard the girl say to her boyfriend, 'Would you still love me if I looked like her?' **FML**

*

Today, my name was called during assembly because I'd won a prize. Everyone booed. **FML**

Today, I was sitting in class and fell asleep during the lesson. I was wearing jogging bottoms and got an erection. My teacher came up to me and grabbed my penis. She thought it was my phone. **FML**

Today, I was walking to my car when I saw a large man walking behind me. I hurried to open my car as he was approaching quickly. My door wasn't unlocking and I panicked. It was then that I noticed it wasn't even my car. As I walked away from the vehicle, he walked up and unlocked the door. **FML**

Today, a fashion supplement called 'Looking Good', about fashion in schools, was published in our local newspaper. The front page featured a picture of my class. I'd been photoshopped out. **FML**

*

Today, I opened my birthday present from my grandfather. It was a map of the USA, colour-coded by regional percentage of available men. **FML**

Today, my mum took me to the doctor. Puberty still hasn't arrived, and the doctor seemed concerned as he examined me. Then he left the room, and left the door ajar. I overheard him discussing my undeveloped penis with my mum, and then he brought her in to show her the 'problem'. **FML**

Today, my daughter asked me how old I was the first time I had sex. After I told her twenty-two, she quickly shouted, 'Beat ya!' She's thirteen. **FML**

*

Today, I dropped my keys. Not wanting to lean over and pick them up, I pointed at them and said, '*Accio*.' I tried to use a *Harry Potter* spell in public. **FML**

Today, it was my final meeting with my psychologist, who was helping me with my bipolar disorder. I just found out that he's committed suicide. **FML**

Today, I went swimming. As I was getting out of the very crowded pool, a little girl ran up to me, pointed, and then yelled, 'Mummy, I want big boobies like that when I grow up!' I'm a boy. **FML**

Today, I was sitting in science class when, to my surprise, I felt my pants suddenly becoming warm and wet. I looked behind me to see that four boys from my class had inserted a small funnel into my exposed bum crack and poured the melted butter from the experiment into it. **FML**

*

Today, my cat was in the bathroom with me. I was getting undressed to get into the shower. My cat looked at me after I'd undressed and then proceeded to throw up all over the rug. **FML**

*

Today, I was excited because I finally received responses from all the applications I'd made to various universities. I put the letters in the order of my preference before opening them. Didn't get into my first choice. Denied from my second choice. Rejected from my third choice. On the waiting list for my back-up. Accepted for a job at Morrisons. **FML**

*

Today, I was masturbating into a sock when I felt something on my cock. I quickly ripped the sock off and threw it on the floor. A huge spider came scurrying out. **FML**

*

Today, I went for a jog. While I was running, I passed my girlfriend's parents, who were out for a walk. Trying to make a good impression, I stopped to talk. When I got home, I realized I was wearing a shirt that friends had given me as a joke. It said: 'Blow me, bitch. It's my b-day.' **FML**

Today, I was out on a date with a guy. His colleague came to have a beer with us, and I knew my best friend would think he was gorgeous. I wanted to take a picture of him without him knowing, so I held up my phone and pretended to be texting. The flash went off. **FML**

∗

Today is my sixteenth birthday. Thinking that my parents were at work, I decided it would be fun to sunbathe nude in my back garden. My parents had set up a surprise party. I was standing naked in front of half my school. **FML**

∗

Today, I was diagnosed with pancreatic cancer. I called my family to invite them over this evening. I told them I had some very important news that could not wait. They all declined the invite. When I asked why, they said they were going to my cousin's to watch his new TV. **FML**

∗∗∗

Today, I was discussing my heritage with my girlfriend's family. The minute I told them I came from a German background, her seven-year-old brother pointed at me and yelled, 'Hitler!' **FML**

Today, during dinner, my new girlfriend's father stroked my leg several times under the table with his bare foot. **FML**

Today, I was in a queue at the supermarket. The woman in front of me looked right at me, turned to her friend, and then said, 'That reminds me, I forgot to get acne cream.' **FML**

✱

Today, it's my birthday. My ex just sent me a text. I read it, happy that he had remembered. He wanted me to know he has a new girlfriend. **FML**

✱

Today, I was reading a really good book. With a large chunk of the story still to go, I turned the page and saw, handwritten at the top, 'Lauren kills Paul in the end … You shouldn't have pissed me off.' It was from my sister – we had a fight yesterday. **FML**

Today, I was swimming in the ocean with my best friend when a giant wave came and knocked off the bottom half of my bikini. My friend told me that she would go and get me a replacement swimsuit so that I could walk onto the very crowded beach. She left me for half an hour, laughing from the shore with her entire family. **FML**

Today, I sent a text message to my ex-boyfriend, who dumped me four months ago, asking him to come back. His reply: 'Feeling-wise, I won't come back to you, but sexually, why not?' **FML**

Today, I was on a train, sitting next to an old man who was reading a newspaper. Suddenly, he sneezed, without putting his hands over his nose. Instead of turning towards the window, he turned towards me. **FML**

*

Today, my fiancé told me that, after seven years together, he is no longer in love with me. Shocked and appalled, I asked him if he had anything else to add. 'Happy Birthday.' **FML**

*

Today, my best friend invited me to dinner at his house. When I went to the bathroom, I found my wife's wedding ring, which she'd lost a week ago. **FML**

*

Today, my boss called me into his office to tell me I had got a pay rise. Excited, I went out and bought a new Chanel bag. Two hours later, he called me in again – to tell me he'd been kidding. **FML**

*

Today, my boss told me that we are having a big meeting tomorrow with lots of important people. Before leaving the room, he added, 'Please, tomorrow, try to dress better.' **FML**

*

Today, kids were chatting while I was trying to teach a lesson. After three speeches about 'the next person who talks gets a note to take home', one kid looks right at me and goes, 'Miaow.' **FML**

Today, at lunch, I ordered a Coke. When the waiter read back my order, he said, 'Diet Coke,' so I corrected him, saying, 'No, regular Coke.' He shook his head and said again, 'Diet Coke.' **FML**

*

Today, a woman in a shop stopped me and told me loudly that if I bought her product, it would get rid of my acne. **FML**

*

Today, I was putting in a new light bulb when my wife walked into the room and said, 'You can't see a thing, I'll turn the light on for you.' And she did, electrocuting me. **FML**

*

Today, my five-year-old daughter watched me getting dressed in the bathroom and asked, 'Mum, when my boobs grow, will they droop like yours?' **FML**

*

Today, a colleague asked me if I had a comb he could borrow. I'm bald. **FML**

*

Today, my man and I were having sex on the edge of the bed. We were using chocolate spread and I was riding him. When it was over, he got up and I noticed a long brown line on the edge of the bed. I knelt down to smell it. It wasn't chocolate. **FML**

*

Today, my husband called me 'my little zebra'. I gave birth a month ago, and I've got a few stretch marks. **FML**

Today, the ugliest girl in school walked by me and said, 'Eww.' **FML**

Today, my mother bought me Mickey Mouse-shaped burgers for my dinner. I'm twenty-two. **FML**

Today, while we were watching TV together, my boyfriend elbowed me in the ribs and smiled meaningfully at me during an ad for a weight-loss product. **FML**

✱

Today, my mum asked me for advice on how to give a good blow job. I'm a bloke. **FML**

✱

Today, the guy I've secretly been in love with for years told me how hot my brother is. **FML**

Today, I was lying in bed with my boyfriend.
He grabbed my double chin and said,
'Gobble, gobble.' **FML**

*

Today, I figured I'd give my boyfriend a
compliment, and told him how 'gifted' he was
below the belt. In return, he told me how much
he loves that little roll of fat that pops up over the
top of my trousers when I sit down. I'm trying to
lose weight. **FML**

*

Today, I have to be at work with a smile on my
face, while sitting next to the arsehole who
dumped me last week. **FML**

*

Today, I told my mum that I want to get
liposuction. She said, 'What's the point? You
can't get lipo on your face.' **FML**

*

Today, my boyfriend showed his mother some
photos of me. She thought that I looked like a
celebrity from her home country of Korea.
Flattered, I googled this celebrity. She is a porn
star who's had cosmetic surgery. **FML**

*

Today, I sent out my CV to about a dozen
prospective employers. Afterwards, I realized that
I hadn't updated it for a while so I went to look
over it, to see what I could add. My ex had
changed my objective to: 'I'm a cocksucker
who desperately needs a job.' **FML**

Today, I went to the doctor to talk about my depression and low self-esteem. He told me that I shouldn't think of myself as a fat pig for being overweight. I didn't think I was overweight. **FML**

✱

Today, I asked my mum how much she had set aside for my university fees. She looked at me as if I were crazy and said, 'Why the hell would I do anything like that?' **FML**

✱

Today, I went out to eat with my aunt and uncle. I barely looked at the cute waiter because I'm a terribly shy person. Then my uncle exclaimed to him, 'You should take out my niece! She's never dated in her life.' I'm twenty-eight. **FML**

Today, I was playing with three kids I look after. The middle one has just learned about sex and started chanting that I had done it with the eldest as a joke. We were in the garden and the neighbours heard. I've been fired, escorted off the premises and I am now being investigated by the police. **FML**

Today, at work, I was refilling some guy's tea, and the uppity jerk had the gall to ask me if I'd ever kissed a girl considering how fat I am, how high my voice is, and how little money I make. **FML**

Today, I was complaining to my sister about how jealous I was of her looks. Her response was: 'Sometimes it's OK to be the ugly sister. Like, you have less chance of getting raped.' **FML**

*

Today, I came into work with a new haircut and everyone asked me if I lost a bet. **FML**

*

Today, I woke up next to a slumbering girl I had just met the night before. She had all the covers on top of her and I was cold. Not only was I cold, but the sheets beneath me were also really cold. And damp. So I got up – and realized she'd peed all over my bed. **FML**

*

Today, I told my girlfriend that I didn't feel wanted. Then she proceeded to talk about how her cat had puked on the carpet. **FML**

Today, I was sitting at home, venting to my parents about how I never get asked out by any of the guys at school. My dad's words of wisdom were: 'Don't worry, looks don't matter so much in college. Once they've got a few beers in them, they'll date anything.' **FML**

Today, my girlfriend gave me a blow-up doll and told me to practise. **FML**

Today, I realized it's been five days since my boyfriend last answered his phone when I called. Two weeks ago, he told me he used to break up with his girlfriends in a very juvenile way. He didn't answer their phone calls. **FML**

*

Today, my wife left me the following voicemail: 'Alex, last night was amazing. You took me to places I've never been to before. I can't wait to see you tonight after work.' My name is Rob. We haven't had sex in two years. **FML**

*

Today, I got a text message. It said: 'I'm so drunk. What you up to, girl?' It was from my dad. **FML**

Today, I decided to come out to a colleague. She looked at me, then laughed and said, 'You can't be gay, you're fat!' **FML**

Today, I went on a first date with a guy I met at a speed-dating event. He recommended the lamb shank, which I proceeded to order without looking at the menu. When the waiter took my order, my date said, 'Wait, the lamb is £27, why don't you get the chicken?' He then ordered the lamb for himself. **FML**

*

Today, I sang at a retirement home with my school choir. Afterwards, we went to speak to the elderly people, just to get to know them a little. The first woman I met asked, 'Are you a boy or a girl?' **FML**

*

Today, I texted my boyfriend saying hi. His response: 'I got your best friend pregnant.' **FML**

*

Today, my mother and I got into a huge fight about me being a lesbian. It ended with me saying, 'Fuck you!' to which she responded: 'I bet you'd probably like to.' **FML**

*

Today, I wore a new striped shirt to work. One of my colleagues said to me, 'I like your shirt. Most fat people don't look good in horizontals.' **FML**

*

Today, I heard my sister masturbating in her room. I took the dog for a quick walk to get out of the house, and came back to see her leaving her room … my electric toothbrush in her hand. **FML**

Today, I went to get my school picture taken.
The photographer looked at me and said,
'You look like you need a mirror.' **FML**

✱

Today, I was teaching in a school. One kid messed
up my hair. I said, 'Why'd you do that?' He said,
'I have lice, now you have lice too!' **FML**

✱

Today, I got my boyfriend a pair of concert tickets
for his birthday. He loved the gift, but turned to
me and said, 'Do I have to take you?' **FML**

✱

Today, my ex-boyfriend came over. After I
finished pouring my heart out to him about how
much I missed him and how much I loved him,
he looked at me and asked, 'So are we gonna
do it, or what?' **FML**

✱

Today, I told my mum I was going through a
growth spurt. She said, 'Yeah, horizontally.' **FML**

✱

Today, we wrote Valentine's Day poems in class.
I wrote a very depressing poem about how I was
rejected by all the girls I like and how it hurt to
be alone. When it was read to the class, they
laughed and told me it was hilarious. Even
the teacher. **FML**

✱

Today, I went for a coffee with a guy I'm
interested in. He picked up his phone mid-date
to finalize dinner plans with another girl. **FML**

Today, I jokingly had a sexual conversation via text message with a good male friend. He was pretending to be a stranger and was fishing for compliments and asking to have a foursome. Turns out, my friend had lost his phone. I spent two hours talking to a random pervert about what lingerie I was wearing. **FML**

*

Today, as I sat on my couch, heartbroken after a very recent break-up, my mother walked up to me and said in a comforting voice, 'Maybe he left you for someone else.' **FML**

Today, I was at a club and the DJ said, 'Turn to the person next to you and picture them naked, then drink a beer if the mental image disturbs you.' I turned, only to find myself face to face with my ex-boyfriend. He drank two beers. **FML**

Today, I went alone to a fast-food restaurant to pick up food for a work party. I ordered 250 chicken fingers, fifteen orders of fries and two gallons of tea, and the guy behind the counter asked, 'Is this for here or to take out?' **FML**

*

Today, my flatmate walked into my room and asked, 'So ... when are you leaving?' She was throwing a party in our apartment. I wasn't invited. **FML**

Today, my boyfriend and I were making out while watching a movie. Just as I was getting really into it, he told me to move my head. He couldn't see the television. **FML**

*

Today, I went to McDonald's for lunch and ordered a salad. The man behind the counter looked at me and said, 'Well, at least you're trying.' **FML**

*

Today, I was trying on lingerie in a changing room with my boyfriend next to me. I told him in a seductive, playful tone, 'You can stay and watch if you give me a piece of your gum.' He said, 'Nope, I only have three left,' and walked out. **FML**

*

Today, I had sex for the first time with a guy. After he had passionately made love to me, I turned to him and said, 'You smell really good.' He turned to me and said, 'You don't.' **FML**

Today, I returned home from uni and saw a framed picture of my parents and my younger sister on an elephant in the jungle. I pointed to the picture and asked my mum, 'Is this some photoshop job?' She responded, 'No, we went to Thailand for a family trip – didn't we tell you?' **FML**

Today, I was eating in a restaurant with my boyfriend. He is six foot two and I'm four foot eleven. Out of nowhere, the waitress started openly flirting with him, and asked him if he needed a booster chair for his daughter. **FML**

Today, I called my boyfriend, crying, to tell him I'd had the most terrible day. He said I should come over and he would make me feel better. I said I just wanted to snuggle, and I was impressed with his sincerity. Then he said, 'Can we snuggle ... with my dick in you?' **FML**

Today, I went to chill with my best friend and his girlfriend, whom I recently met after I moved to the area. After a few beers, my mate leaned over and tried to kiss me. I quickly backed off and looked over at his girlfriend, expecting the same shocked reaction. She winked. **FML**

*

Today, I complimented my mum: 'Hey, I think you've lost some weight.' She replied, 'Yeah, I think you found it.' **FML**

*

Today, my mum decided to give me relationship advice. She told me the key to a happy/successful relationship was 'letting your man explore all your orifices'. **FML**

Today, I was playing basketball with my little brother. After I jokingly blocked his shot, he turned to me and said, 'You're a bitch.' He's six. I asked him where he'd heard that word. He replied, 'Daddy calls you that when you're not around.' **FML**

Today, my grandmother told me that not only does she not accept me as a homosexual man, but she also feels my relationship with a little person is 'spitting in God's face'. **FML**

Today, I woke up to find that my dog was missing. I'd spent about an hour searching for him when my psycho ex-girlfriend texted me his photo. She'd kidnapped him. After driving over there, she shot paintballs at my car. Now I have no dog and a colourful car. **FML**

*

Today, I met a guy in a bar and we went back to my apartment. We started having sex. About thirty seconds in, he stops and says it's not right – he likes me too much for a one-night stand. He gives me his number, a kiss on the cheek and leaves. He'd already come. I called his phone. Wrong number. **FML**

*

Today, my brother joked that our dog was more attractive than I was. I looked to my mum for support, and she said, 'Well, she is pure bred.' **FML**

*

Today, I returned from a half-month-long trip to China with a group of friends. I threw myself into my mother's arms and burst into tears, but she stopped me to say, 'Listen ... these last couple of weeks have been some of the best I've ever had. Can we try to keep it like that?' **FML**

*

Today, I wanted to have a good lunch with my wife before fasting for my surgery, which I may not survive – but she decided getting her hair cut was more important. I ate alone. **FML**

Today, I went to the doctor with my parents.
When the doctor asked if I was sexually active,
I said yes. My mum laughed and said, 'Good one.'
My dad, for added effect, said, 'Your hand
doesn't count.' **FML**

*

Today, I saw my mum sneaking meat into her
spaghetti sauce. She proceeded to tell me that
she sneaks meat into most of the food she cooks.
I've been a vegetarian for eight years. **FML**

*

Today, I was feeling really upset and called my
boyfriend. He said, 'Can you feel upset a little
later? I'm watching a movie.' **FML**

*

Today, I went to get a condom from my drawer
because my boyfriend and I were going to have
sex for the first time. When I opened the drawer, I
saw that every single condom had a pin stabbed
through it, and there was a note on top of the
box: 'Love Mum.' **FML**

*

Today, I kissed my girlfriend and she tasted like a
cigarette. I don't smoke. She doesn't smoke. My
flatmate does. **FML**

*

Today, my boyfriend called me from a payphone
because he'd lost his phone at the airport. When I
texted his phone to get a response from whoever
had stolen it, I received a message back saying,
'Love the pics. Send more ;-).' **FML**

Today, I was discussing sex with some of my male friends and I asked one of them what he would do if I got naked and got in his bed. He replied, 'Nothing. You're one of the guys now.' They all agreed. **FML**

✳

Today, I came home to tell my parents about the nose job I had done about a month ago. My mum had always told me I should get one, so I didn't tell her right away to see if she would notice. I was home for about twenty minutes before she asked me, 'So, when are you getting that nose job?' **FML**

Today, I was at my ex-girlfriend's house. I still have a major crush on her. After cuddling as we watched a movie, she began to show me several pictures she had taken of herself on her phone, and asked me which ones I liked the best. She then sent the pictures I had chosen to a guy she met a week ago. **FML**

Today, I was talking to my mum. During the conversation, she randomly asked me, 'Does he take his leg off when you guys are having sex?' referring to the guy I've been seeing, who has a prosthetic leg. My dad then asked, 'Does he beat you with it if you've been naughty?' **FML**

Today, I knew my girlfriend was having a bad day so I went to her office with some flowers. When I was in the lift, I overheard her colleague saying that the reason she was upset was because she had been cheating on her boyfriend. **FML**

*

Today, my sister asked if she could look through my closet to find something to wear. She is six months pregnant. **FML**

*

Today, my boyfriend said that being with me was his payment for past sins. **FML**

*

Today, my boyfriend and I decided to try anal sex. When he'd finished, I turned around to see him holding a strap-on. With a smile on his face, he said, 'Now, do me.' **FML**

*

Today, I had a performance evaluation meeting with my boss. He told me I was the best in my department, and that productivity had never been higher. He went on to say that because everything's working so well, they don't need me as much, so he's cutting my hours. **FML**

*

Today, an elderly gentleman walked into my workplace and asked to use the laminating machine. I explained to him that we kept it behind the counter and I would do it for him, at which point he produced several graphic photos of him having sex with nasty-looking women. **FML**

Today, my girlfriend was packing for her study abroad programme. I jokingly got her a box of condoms. She laughed, saying, 'Oh yeah, I'll definitely need some of those.' I later showed up to take her to the airport and saw her open suitcase in the kitchen, with the condoms on top. **FML**

Today, while at work, I was reading *The Very Hungry Caterpillar* to a class of five-year-olds. I got near the end of the book and said, 'Look at the big fat caterpillar.' One of my pupils replied, 'Just like you!' **FML**

Today, I flew to New Zealand to surprise my girlfriend on her trip. At Auckland Airport, I got a text message saying she wanted to break up with me. I just spent £1,000 on this romantic surprise. **FML**

Today, my grandmother patched up my vintage, limited-edition designer jeans because she thought I'd accidentally ripped them. **FML**

✱

Today, I went to my boyfriend's workplace to surprise him. When I got there, I called him on his mobile to tell him to turn around. I saw him look at his phone and not pick up. His colleague next to him asked who it was. He replied, 'Just this fat bird I know.' **FML**

✱

Today, I found out that my mother has another new boyfriend. She told me she wanted me to meet him, so I reluctantly agreed. When I walked into the living room, to my surprise I already knew him. He's eighteen, my mother is forty-four. He also happens to attend my school. We have a maths class together. **FML**

✱

Today, my family and I were going on a weekend trip. They were supposed to pick me up on the way. About an hour before they were due to arrive, my mum called to tell me that there was no room left in the car, so they wouldn't be stopping to get me. **FML**

✱

Today, my mum had my girlfriend and I over. Out of the blue, she pulled out my grandmother's wedding ring and gave it to me, saying I could now propose. My girlfriend started screaming and said yes. I have been seeing someone else for three months and was going to break up with her. **FML**

Today, I was over at a friend's place until very late. He had stolen my keys as a joke at some point, but by the time I noticed, he was too drunk to remember where he'd hidden them. **FML**

*

Today, at work, a woman came up to my checkout and when I greeted her, she said, 'Oh, you are so beautiful!' I immediately smiled and thanked her – then she looked at me and said, 'Oh, not you,' and pointed to her ear. She was on her phone. **FML**

*

Today, I drove home from a friend's house. I called my folks en route to let them know I was on my way. My dad picked up and in a panting voice said, 'Now isn't a good time – drive around the block for fifteen minutes.' **FML**

*

Today, my girlfriend and I were being driven home from our date by her mother. She's Jewish and I'm Catholic. Her mother was talking about how my girlfriend was going on a trip to Jerusalem that summer. She finished with, 'And you can find a nice Jewish boy while you're there.' **FML**

*

Today, the fitting room of the shop I work in smelled really bad. The customers started to complain and since I was on fitting-room duty, I went to investigate. A middle-aged woman had pooed on the floor and put the chair on top to cover it. **FML**

Today, I received a card in the post. It was from my vet's office. Written inside was: 'We send our sympathy during this trying time.' I haven't been home for three days. I can't find my dog and my mother won't talk about it. My dog was seven. She hated that dog. **FML**

*

Today, I flew home early from a two-month trip to Europe to surprise my boyfriend on his birthday. When I got to his house with a home-made cake and a handmade quilt with silk-screened pictures from my trip, his flatmate answered the door and said, 'Oh sorry, he's out with his girlfriend.' **FML**

*

Today, I was teasing my little brother. Tonight, while I was brushing my teeth, my little brother slips a photo under the door that shows him scrubbing my toothbrush against his nuts. **FML**

*

Today, as I was packing bags at the supermarket, I looked down to see a six-year-old urinating on my shoes and the floor next to me. I told his mother that she should take her kid to the toilets, only to be told to 'mind my own damn business'. I was later fired for arguing with the customer. **FML**

*

Today, my boyfriend and I went out to eat. The waiter came to take our order. My boyfriend said he wanted a cheeseburger. I ordered the same. My boyfriend looked at me and asked, 'Are you sure you don't want a salad?' **FML**

Today, someone stole my phone at a concert.
They thought it would be funny to text my mother
that I was pregnant. **FML**

*

Today, my mum decided to give me a solid reason
for not having premarital sex. She told me that
my future husband will want me to be tight for
our first time. My mum and I were on a ski lift.
The ride lasted ten more uncomfortable minutes.
FML

*

Today, my mother and I went to buy some
sanitary towels. I suggested I get tampons
instead, so that I can go swimming at my
boyfriend's cottage. My mother then goes to the
nearest store employee and asks, 'Excuse me, if
my daughter uses a tampon, does that mean she
is no longer a virgin?' **FML**

*

Today, my white mother-in-law called our house
phone. Since I'm Chilean and have a fairly heavy
accent, she mistook me for the cleaning lady and
scolded me for answering the phone. Before I
could correct her, she said, 'This is why only
white people should be allowed in America,' and
hung up. **FML**

*

Today, my mother told me that she needed a
urine sample from me to send in to the doctors to
test for any allergies. I did what she asked and
then went to my room. I came downstairs later –
and found her in the bathroom, putting my pee on
a pregnancy-test stick. **FML**

Today, I had drunken sex with a girl that I barely know. I didn't have a condom and was nervous about getting her pregnant, but she assured me that I could pull out. Right when I was about to withdraw, she wrapped her legs around me and yelled, 'BE MY BABY'S DADDY!' I couldn't get out in time. **FML**

✱

Today, I was in my back garden scolding my cat. I yelled, 'If you can't learn to use the toilet correctly then I am going to leave you out here in the snow until you figure it out!' Later, my neighbour left me a nasty note about child abuse. **FML**

Today, I was at work and a very obese woman came in to get a pedicure. When she took her shoes off, I noticed an odd black substance on her feet. I started scrubbing it off and wondered out loud, 'What is this stuff?' As a chunk of it fell into my hands, she replied, 'Girl, that's just the fungus.' **FML**

Today, I went to the supermarket with my mum. At the checkout I was eating a bag of crisps while my mum bought her stuff. I inhaled while eating and I started to choke. The cashier asked me if I was OK. My mum just waved her hand, and said, 'Sometimes she does that for attention, ignore her.' **FML**

Today, my flatmate got mad at me for putting away the tampons that were sitting on her desk. She rebelled by hanging hundreds of tampons – dyed red – from every surface in our apartment. I discovered this while giving my mum her first tour of the place. **FML**

*

Today, my boyfriend and I were about to have sex. Just as things were heating up, my wardrobe door flew open and my little brother ran out screaming, 'Mum, they're doing it, come quick!' My mum paid my nine-year-old brother to spy on me. **FML**

*

Today, I'd just finished having dinner with my boyfriend, so I leaned over to him and said seductively, 'How about some dessert?' He looked at me and said, 'Babe, you really don't need it.' **FML**

Today, my girlfriend came up behind me and put her hand in my back pocket. I thought it was someone trying to take my wallet. I elbowed her in the nose and broke it. **FML**

Today, I got a cab home from the airport. The taxi driver was on the phone and not really paying attention. I paid him and got out of the cab, but he drove away before I could get my luggage out of the boot. **FML**

Today, I decided to tell my mum about my choice to wait to have sex until after marriage. Coming from a very Christian family, I thought she would be proud. Instead she laughed and said, 'Is that your excuse for not being able to get laid?' and walked out of the room. **FML**

✱

Today, I asked my parents if the outfit I was wearing made me look fat. My mum looked at me and paused for a while. Then my dad said, 'Honey, that outfit doesn't make you look fat. Your fat makes you look fat.' **FML**

✱

Today, I turned twenty-two without anyone wishing me 'Happy Birthday'. In fact, the only phone call I received all day was from my brother. He wanted to borrow money. **FML**

Today, my mother finally had her beloved Siamese cat cremated. The cat has been dead for over a week and she has been keeping it on her bed, stroking its fur and saying, 'She looks like she's sleeping' and 'She's so cold.' To top it all off, she's been calling me by the cat's name for three years. **FML**

Today, I woke up to the sound of scissors. My mum was cutting my hair while I was asleep. **FML**

Today, my Christian boyfriend of six months broke up with me. I had told him when we started dating that I was an atheist, but he had only just decided to look up what an atheist is. He gave me a Bible. **FML**

*

Today, I found out that my boyfriend owns and wears more thongs than I do. **FML**

Today, I had one of my worst panic attacks in years. I was worried nobody cared about me and that I had completely messed up my life. I was hyperventilating and crying hysterically. My mum walked by my room, looked at me and said, 'If you're going to make those noises, at least shut the door.' **FML**

*

Today, while lying in bed with my girlfriend, she was grabbing my stomach and I told her to stop touching my fat. She replied, 'So don't touch you at all?' **FML**

*

Today, I discovered my eighteen-year-old son has been peeing on the carpet when he is too lazy to get out of bed in the morning – and blaming it on the cat. **FML**

*

Today, I was in the car with my husband, complaining about the way I look. His response: 'Babe, if I cared about the way you looked, I wouldn't have married you.' **FML**

*

Today, after four years of anorexia and lots of recovery, my parents took me, my counsellor and my whole family out to dinner to celebrate my progress. I ended up eating something that made me vomit everything I ate. My parents now think I am bulimic and are sending me back to counselling. **FML**

*

Today, I found a bone in my veggie burger. **FML**

Today, I went on a roller coaster for the first time.
I sat at the back, which was a bad idea. When it
ended, everyone in front of me turned around and
stared. When I asked my friend what was going
on, she said I had been screaming the Lord's
Prayer the whole time. I hadn't even noticed.
FML

*

Today, my boyfriend came over so that we could
have some 'fun'. Turns out, his idea of foreplay
is squishing my breasts together and making
them talk. **FML**

*

Today, my girlfriend dumped me for someone
else. An hour earlier, I had gotten permission
from her dad to propose. **FML**

*

Today, I realized that my life is so boring
I could not think of a single thing to
complain about. **FML**

✱✱✱